297.93
Hartz,
Baha'i Faith

W9-AKD-368

$40.00
ocn261342771
3rd ed.   08/05/2009

WORLD RELIGIONS
BAHA'I FAITH
THIRD EDITION

WORLD RELIGIONS

African Traditional Religion
Baha'i Faith
Buddhism
Catholicism & Orthodox Christianity
Confucianism
Daoism
Hinduism
Islam
Judaism
Native American Religions
Protestantism
Shinto
Sikhism
Zoroastrianism

WORLD RELIGIONS
BAHA'I FAITH
THIRD EDITION

by
Paula Hartz
Series Editors: Joanne O'Brien and Martin Palmer

CHELSEA HOUSE
PUBLISHERS
An imprint of Infobase Publishing

Chelsea House
An imprint of Infobase Publishing
132 West 31st Street
New York NY 10001

Library of Congress Cataloging-in-Publication Data
Hartz, Paula.
 Baha'i Faith / by Paula Hartz. — 3rd ed.
    p. cm. — (World religions)
 Includes bibliographical references and index.
 ISBN 978-1-60413-104-8 (alk. paper)
 1. Bahai Faith. I. Title. II. Series.

 BP365.H323 2009
 297.9'3—dc22

       2008043045

Chelsea House books are available at special discounts when purchased in bulk quantities for businesses, associations, institutions, or sales promotions. Please call our Special Sales Department in New York at (212) 967-8800 or (800) 322-8755.

You can find Chelsea House on the World Wide Web at http://www.chelseahouse.com

This book was produced for Chelsea House by Bender Richardson White, Uxbridge, U.K.
Project Editor: Lionel Bender
Text Editor: Ronne Randall
Designer: Ben White
Picture Researchers: Joanne O'Brien and Kim Richardson
Maps and symbols: Stefan Chabluk

Printed in China

CP BRW 10 9 8 7 6 5 4 3 2 1

This book is printed on acid-free paper.

All links and Web addresses were checked and verified to be correct at the time of publication. Because of the dynamic nature of the Web, some addresses and links may have changed since publication and may no longer be valid.

CONTENTS

PREFACE

Almost from the start of civilization, more than 10,000 years ago, religion has shaped human history. Today more than half the world's population practice a major religion or indigenous spiritual tradition. In many 21st-century societies, including the United States, religion still shapes people's lives and plays a key role in politics and culture. And in societies throughout the world increasing ethnic and cultural diversity has led to a variety of religions being practiced side by side. This makes it vital that we understand as much as we can about the world's religions.

The World Religions series, of which this book is a part, sets out to achieve this aim. It is written and designed to appeal to both students and general readers. The books offer clear, accessible overviews of the major religious traditions and institutions of our time. Each volume in the series describes where a particular religion is practiced, its origins and history, its central beliefs and important rituals, and its contributions to world civilization. Carefully chosen photographs complement the text, and sidebars, a map, fact file, glossary, bibliography, and index are included to help readers gain a more complete understanding of the subject at hand.

These books will help clarify what religion is all about and reveal both the similarities and differences in the great spiritual traditions practiced around the world today.

Countries in Which the Baha'i Faith
Has Established a Presence

1–3.5%

0.1–0.9%

less than 0.1%

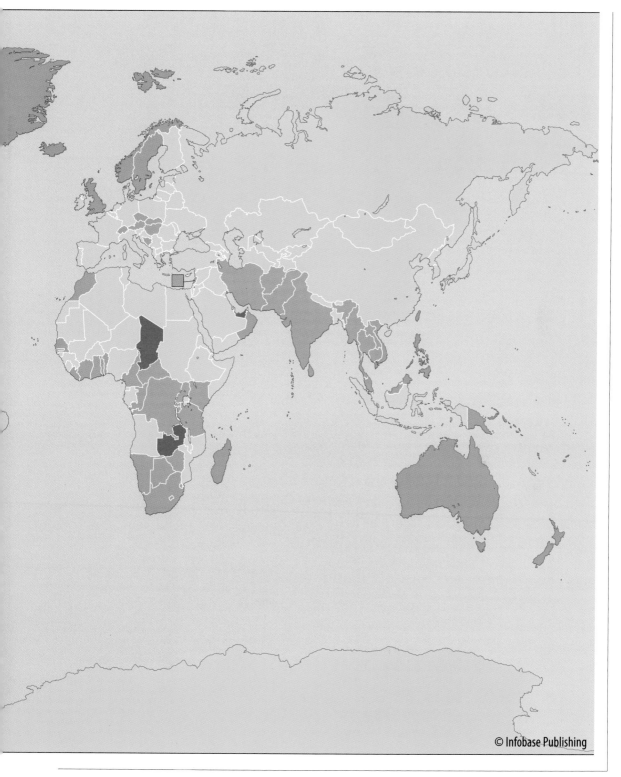

© Infobase Publishing

CHAPTER 1

INTRODUCTION: THE BAHA'I FAITH AND ITS PEOPLE

The Baha'i Faith is the youngest of all independent world religions. It began as a small, local religious movement in Persia (now Iran) less than 200 years ago. Today the Baha'i Faith has some 5 million followers. It is one of the world's fastest-growing religions. It is also probably the most diverse. It has members from every religion, race, ethnic background, nationality, and creed in the world.

DISTRIBUTION

Compared with world religions such as Christianity and Islam, each of which has more than a billion followers, the Baha'i Faith is relatively small. However, according to the Baha'i World Center (the spiritual and administrative center in northern Israel), Baha'is have established communities in virtually every country and territory around the world, making it the world's second most widespread religion after Christianity. It represents more than 2,100 ethnic, racial, and tribal groups. Baha'is live in more than 100,000 localities. There are organized Baha'i communities with elected local councils, called spiritual assemblies, in more than 10,000

The Baha'i house of worship in New Delhi, India, built in 1986. It is known as the Lotus Temple because of its striking design. It is one of the most visited tourist attractions in the world.

towns or localities There are national or regional elected bodies in 182 countries.

The Baha'i Faith spread to North America in the last years of the 19th century. In the past hundred years it has spread to nearly every country and territory in the world. The largest Baha'i communities are in South Asia, Africa, and Latin America, as well as in some Pacific islands, but India has the largest single Baha'i community. That country has more than 1 million Baha'i followers, although that is still a small proportion of the total Indian population. In the United States there are approximately 165,000 members of the Baha'i Faith.

THE MIDDLE EAST TODAY

At the time of the foundation of the Baha'i Faith in Persia (the area that became modern Iran in 1925), the Arabian Peninsula, the Middle East, and surrounding areas were part of the Ottoman Empire. This was undergoing a period of great upheaval and change.

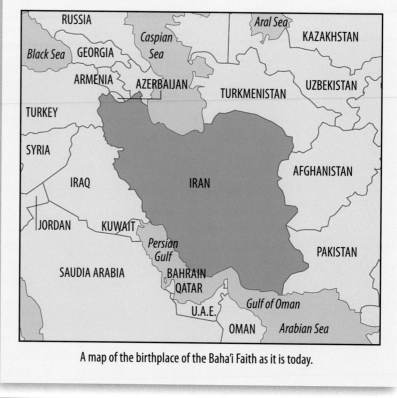

A map of the birthplace of the Baha'i Faith as it is today.

CENTRAL FIGURES OF THE BAHA'I FAITH

The Baha'i Faith traces its beginnings in Persia to a religious leader called the Bab ["the Gate"] (1819–50). In 1844 the Bab announced that he had had a revelation from God and that he was a bearer of divine truth. People began to follow him. The Muslim religious leaders of Persia felt threatened by this new movement and its ability to attract followers. They persecuted the Bab and his followers. They had him arrested, beaten, and imprisoned. Finally he was executed by a firing squad for the crime of heresy since the Bab's followers presented his words as the newly revealed words of God. Many of his followers we also killed.

BAHA'IS AROUND THE WORLD

This piechart shows the distrubution of the followers of the Baha'i Faith by continents of the world.

Asia has the largest Baha'i population.

BAHA'IS IN THE UNITED STATES

Number of Baha'i followers	about 165,000
Number of localities where Baha'is reside	about 10,000
Number of local spiritual assemblies	about 1,200
Baha'i schools and institutions	6

Shoghi Effendi Rabbani as a child. As Guardian of the Faith, Shoghi Effendi (1897–1957) translated Baha'i writings and created special plans to spread the faith to many different continents.

The person who gave the Baha'i Faith its special character and shaped its spiritual and moral values is known as Baha'u'llah (1817–92). He was one of the Bab's early followers, but his importance is so great that in Baha'i tradition the Bab is often considered his precursor. While Baha'u'llah was in prison for participating in the Babi movement, he had a vision. He understood that God had called on him to be a divine messenger of God's word. He took the name Baha'u'llah, which means "Glory of God." After the Bab's death, Baha'u'llah rallied the Bab's followers. They gave themselves the name Baha'i—"followers of Baha."

Because Baha'u'llah was born a nobleman and had connections to the court of the shah, the Persian king, he escaped the Bab's fate, not least because the Babi massacres had provoked vigorous protests from the British and Russian embassies. However he was banished from Persia and spent most of the rest of his life in exile and many years in prison.

When Baha'u'llah died in 1892 his will appointed his son 'Abdu'l-Baha (1844–1921) leader of the faith. He continued his father's work, strengthening and organizing the young religion. On 'Abdu'l-Baha's death in 1921 he left a will naming his grandson, Shoghi Effendi Rabbani (1897–1957), to succeed him as Guardian of the Faith. Shoghi Effendi created special plans that spread the faith to many different countries. He also translated and interpreted many of his grandfather's and great-grandfather's writings.

Shoghi Effendi died in 1957 without leaving an heir. The leadership of the faith passed to the Hands of the Cause of God, a group of Baha'i leaders Shoghi Effendi had named earlier to help him in his work. In 1963 this interim arrangement ended when Baha'is elected the Universal House of Justice, an institution that was originally planned and described by Baha'u'llah, to lead the faith in the future.

PROGRESSIVE REVELATION

Baha'is believe in one God and creator but they understand that they cannot fully know God. God is infinite and the human mind is finite. People know God because throughout history God has sent divine messengers to the world to teach people God's will for them. These divine teachers are part of God's plan for humanity. They came to teach people about God and to move the human race toward greater spiritual, moral, and intellectual truth.

MESSENGERS OF THE ONE GOD

Among the divine messengers are Abraham and Moses of Judaism, Krishna of Hinduism, Zarathushtra of Zoroastrianism, Gautama Buddha of Buddhism, Jesus of Christianity, and the prophet Muhammad of Islam. Baha'is believe that all the leaders and founders of the great religions are equally messengers of the one God. The Baha'i position is best summed up in this statement from the Universal House of Justice published in "One Common Faith" in 2005: "God is one and, beyond all diversity of cultural expression and human interpretation, religion is likewise one . . . . Religion is religion as science is science. Baha'is believe

NINE-POINTED STAR

A nine-pointed star is the symbol of the Baha'i Faith. The number 9 is significant to Baha'is. Baha'u'llah received his revelation nine years after the Bab received his. As the highest single-digit number, 9 symbolizes completeness. Baha'i temples are nine-sided, in recognition of that completeness.

that each of the divine messengers throughout history brought truth and understanding that was right for a particular place and time in the world. The moral and spiritual values they taught helped civilization to advance. The continuing advancement of humanity is part of God's great plan."

Children at a school run by Baha'ís. Education of children is a religious duty in the Baha'i Faith. Many schools have children from a wide range of backgrounds and nationalities, reflecting Baha'u'llah's teachings that all humanity is one race.

THE TIME FOR WORLDWIDE UNITY

Today we live in a very different world from that of leaders like the Buddha, Jesus, or the prophet Muhammad. Although their teachings are still valid, we have reached a new, broader understanding of the world. The world is coming of age. We can see that we all live on one planet and that its future depends on global actions.

Political, environmental, and social problems in one place are no longer isolated events; they affect the whole world. Baha'u'llah taught that this is the era for a single, unified faith with a global viewpoint. Baha'is see Baha'u'llah as the divine messenger for the modern age.

Baha'is do not worship Baha'u'llah as a divine being, but they revere him as a great teacher. His writings are considered divine revelation given by the one God. Baha'is also understand that in time God will send yet more messengers to guide humanity. Baha'u'llah will not be the last. He promised that another messenger would come after him, after 1,000 years. Baha'u'llah's message to the world is simple and straightforward: Now is the time for worldwide unity. People must learn to get along with one another. They must begin to think globally. "The world is but one country, and mankind its citizens," he says.

SPIRITUAL BELIEFS

Baha'is believe that all people are spiritual in nature. Each person has a rational and everlasting soul. The soul is the real "self" of each individual. Each person's soul can be seen in his or her character; it shows in love and compassion, in faith and courage, in kindness and understanding.

According to Baha'i belief, the human soul needs spiritual nourishment in order to be fulfilled. The food of the soul is prayer, scripture, love of God, high moral values, and service to humanity. Time on earth should be devoted to developing the qualities that bring people nearer to God.

The Soul Returns to God

Baha'is believe that the soul lives on after death. When the human body dies the soul is released into the world of the spirit, which has neither time nor place. The exact nature of life after death cannot be known, but Baha'u'llah says that death should be a time of great joy, for the soul returns to God.

A WORLD COMMUNITY

One thing that sets the Baha'i Faith apart from other world religions is its uniting perspective. Baha'is are especially diverse and comprise a widespread organization across the world, yet Baha'u'llah taught that as there is only one God, there is only

A SUMMARY OF VIRTUE

Be generous in prosperity and thankful in adversity.
Be worthy of the trust of thy neighbor, and look upon him
with a bright and friendly face.
Be a treasure to the poor,
    an admonisher to the rich,
    an answerer of the cry of the needy,
    a preserver of the sanctity of thy pledge.
Be fair in thy judgment, and guarded in thy speech.
Be unjust to no man, and show all meekness to all men.
Be as a lamp unto them that walk in darkness,
    a joy to the sorrowful,
    a sea for the thirsty,
    a haven for the distressed,
    an upholder and defender of the victim of oppression.
Let integrity and uprightness distinguish all thine acts.
Be a home for the stranger,
    a balm to the suffering,
    a tower of strength for the fugitive.
Be eyes to the blind, and a guiding light unto the feet
of the erring.
Be an ornament to the countenance of truth,
    a crown to the brow of fidelity,
    a pillar to the temple of righteousness,
    a breath of life to the body of mankind,
    an ensign of the hosts of justice,
    a luminary above the horizon of virtue,
    a dew to the soil of the human heart,
    an ark on the ocean of knowledge,
    a sun in the heaven of bounty,
    a gem on the diadem of wisdom,
    a shining light in the firmament of thy generation,
    a fruit on the tree of humility.

(Baha'u'llah, *Gleanings from the Writings of Baha'u'llah*.)

The Invocation symbol is another symbol that appears in Baha'i homes and buildings. It is the phrase *Ya Baha'u'l–Ahba,* or "O Glory of the All–Glorious" in Arabic.

A member of the Baha'i community in Nepal praying. Baha'is read and meditate on their scriptures every day.

one race—the human race. The time has come, he preached, for uniting all people into one society under one faith.

A large number of Baha'is have converted from other faiths. They come from many different, and sometimes conflicting, backgrounds. Formerly, they may have been Christians or Jews, Buddhists, Muslims, Sikhs, Zoroastrians, or Hindus. Others come from African or Native American tribal religions. Some did not previously belong to any religion. Baha'is are not required to renounce their previous beliefs, but to accept a new unfolding of religious understanding that incorporates them. They understand that there is only one religion, and that is faith in God. All religions are therefore expressions of a single divine plan. For Baha'is, their faith fulfills the promises of all earlier beliefs.

Baha'is come from all races and ethnic groups and from different economic and social classes. Their faith forbids prejudice of any kind. They work together to break down barriers of prejudice and to build a global society in which all people live in harmony.

THE BAHA'I FAITH AND THE INDIVIDUAL

The Baha'i Faith places a great deal of responsibility on the individual. Unlike most other religions, it has no clergy. People are expected to read the Baha'i scriptures for themselves and apply the lessons they find there to actions in their own lives. There are no sermons and no liturgy, or set order of worship. Instead Baha'is meet on a regular basis to read scripture, discuss Baha'i issues and projects, and share fellowship. Depending on the size of the community they generally gather in Baha'i centers or in private homes. The Baha'i Faith does have places of worship in more countries in the world than any other religion, except Christianity. One special feature is that on each continent there is a central temple for that continent, often of startlingly beauti-

> **Prayer for Serenity**
>
> *Oh God! Refresh and gladden my spirit. Purify my heart. Illumine my powers. I lay all my affairs in Thy hand. Thou art my Guide and Refuge. I will no longer be full of anxiety, nor will I let trouble harass me. I will not dwell on the unpleasant things of life.*
>
> *O God! Thou art more friend to me than I am to myself. I dedicate myself to Thee, O Lord.*
>
> ('Abdu'l-Baha, *Baha'i Prayers.*)

ful design, such as a lotus flower in Delhi. The local places of worship and the continental temples are open to people of all faiths for meditation.

The Baha'i Faith emphasizes personal development. All people have both a spiritual and a physical nature. While people must satisfy basic physical needs for such things as shelter and food, they must recognize that the only way to be truly happy is to develop their spiritual side. This emphasis on spirit is what makes people truly human. Prayer and meditation open the soul to new possibilities. Being part of a diverse group breaks down prejudice. Baha'is abstain from alcohol and drugs, because these substances deaden the mind and the spirit.

BAHA'I UNITY

Although Baha'is celebrate their diversity, they understand that they must be firmly united in order to achieve their goals. The writings of Baha'u'llah and 'Abdu'l-Baha clearly establish the rules for holding the community together. There is one institution that is the final authority on any disagreements within the faith. That is the Universal House of Justice at the World Center of the Baha'i Faith in Haifa, Israel. This is an elected body that decides all Baha'i issues.

No individual is permitted to claim special understanding of the faith and start a sect. The Baha'i community is unified. As part of their covenant of faith all Baha'is agree to accept the final authority established in the Baha'i scriptures. Compared to other religious texts, the scriptures of the Baha'i Faith are fairly modern. They were personally written or dictated by Baha'u'llah and 'Abdu'l-Baha in the 19th and 20th centuries. Being so recent, the language is relatively clear and easy to follow. Moreover, both Baha'u'llah and 'Abdu'l-Baha devoted many pages of writings explaining doctrine that their followers did not understand. So although Baha'is read the scriptures independently

The Greatest Name symbol.

Baha

The Greatest Name symbol is the word *baha,* or "glory," written in Arabic script. It appears on Baha'i temples and buildings. Baha'is may also wear jewelry engraved with this symbol.

BAHA'I PRINCIPLES

Baha'u'llah left many writings that included the principles by which all humanity should live. His son 'Abdu'l-Baha, who led the faith after his father's death, broadened them. The principles 'Abdu'l-Baha used to introduce the Baha'i Faith to people around the world remain the guidelines for living as a Baha'i:

Each person must independently seek truth for him- or herself.

All divine religions are one. Everyone worships the same God.

Human progress does not occur through material things alone.

Genuine progress comes from spirituality.

Science and reason are in harmony with religion.

The whole human race is one. All human beings are equally the children of God. People must wipe out all prejudices: religious, racial, political, national, and class.

Extremes of wealth and poverty must be abolished.

Women are the equals of men and are to have equality of rights, particlarly of educational opportunity.

All children must receive a basic education.

There should be a single world federation with a single economy and a single language.

and find their own meanings, they abide by the authoritative interpretation of the elected body that is the head of the faith.

BAHA'IS AND SOCIAL POLICY

Baha'is learn that one of the most important ways of developing the spirit is through service to others. Helping other people is a characteristic of true humanity. Baha'is freely volunteer their time and talents to help others. Work also is a form of worship, because it profits both the community and the worker.

An important goal of the Baha'i Faith is promoting the well-being of humankind. Therefore Baha'is are engaged in a wide variety of social and developmental projects around the world. Wherever they go they establish beneficial programs. These programs reflect the particular needs of the local communities. They may be tutorial schools, after-school projects, health clinics, classes in health care, agricultural projects, orphanages, environmental centers and tree-planting programs, vocational programs, women's centers, and many other programs to benefit society. Often a program starts in a Baha'i living room with a Baha'i volunteer and two or three students. All Baha'is understand that teaching and helping others is a fundamental part of practicing their religion in the same way that attending worship might be for someone of another faith.

Baha'is finance these projects on their own. They volunteer their time and resources. Members also support the faith's social efforts with voluntary contributions. The Baha'i Faith does not accept contributions from outside its own membership. It is entirely self-supporting.

THE UNIQUENESS OF THE BAHA'I FAITH

The Baha'i Faith is the only world religion to emerge during the modern age. Most other world religions are many hundreds or even thousands of years old. Judaism dates back more than 5,000 years, and Zoroastrianism more than 3,000 years. Native American and African belief systems are older than recorded time. Buddhism dates back about 2,500 years. Christianity began more than 2,000 years ago, and Islam more than 1,400 years ago. The earliest recorded works in Shinto are well over 1,000 years old. Even Sikhism, the next youngest world religion, is about 500 years old.

The Baha'i Faith's founders lived in modern times. 'Abdu'l-Baha, Baha'u'llah's son, lived to see such things as railroads, the

telegraph and the telephone, automobiles, even airplanes. All the Baha'i founders were literate. They produced volumes of writing, most of which survives. Unlike religions such as Christianity and Judaism, whose scriptures were written perhaps scores or even hundreds of years after the events they describe, Baha'i scripture is composed of the actual words of its founders, most often in their own handwriting.

There are more firsthand accounts of the Baha'i Faith's early years and its struggles, as well as of the people who brought it into existence, than of any other world religion. The Baha'i Faith thus presents a unique opportunity to see and understand how a new religion begins and how it grows and spreads.

Training in the Barli Development Institute for Rural Women in Indore, India. Baha'is run development programs around the world, including women's programs, health clinics, youth programs, and environmental centers.

CHAPTER 2

FOUNDATIONS OF THE BAHA'I FAITH

The Baha'i Faith grew out of religious influences and ideals in 19th-century Persia. Baha'u'llah, the founder of the Baha'i Faith, was born a Muslim. While one important influence on the Baha'i Faith is Islam, both Islamic scholars and Baha'is themselves have rejected the idea that the Baha'i Faith is a branch of Islam. The Baha'i Faith is a separate religion, distinct and different from Islam. However the Baha'i Faith incorporates many Islamic ideals and practices, such as required daily prayer, giving to the poor, pilgrimage, and fasting.

Even more directly, the Baha'i Faith grew out of a religious movement that came immediately before it. This was the Babi Faith, or Babism. Babis were followers of the Bab, a religious leader in Persia from 1844 until 1850. The Baha'i Faith's religious foundations rest on many of the teachings of the Bab, particularly his vision of a new social order and his promise that a new divine messenger was coming soon.

The Arc gardens in Haifa, Israel. The buildings shown are the Seat of the Universal House of Justice, the International Teaching Center Building, the Center for the Study of the Texts, and the International Baha'i Archives.

To understand the Baha'i Faith it helps to know a little bit about the background from which it came: Islam and Babism.

ISLAM COMES TO PERSIA

Islam began in Arabia in the mid-seventh century C.E. About the same time Arab armies conquered Persia, and by 652 a Muslim ruler sat on the Persian throne. Islam swept the Persian populace. By the ninth century Persia was predominately Islamic.

Early in its history Islam divided into two major sects. These were the Sunnis and the Shia, which remain the two major branches of Islam today. In Persia, the birthplace of Baha'u'llah, the most important branch of Islam was Shia. Persian, or Iranian, Islam is known as "Twelver Shia" because of the tradition of the 12 imams, divinely guided leaders and direct descendants of the prophet Muhammad.

In the Shii tradition, when prophet Muhammad died he selected his son-in-law, Ali, to lead the faithful. Ali in turn passed the leadership down to his descendants. These chosen leaders were known as imams. Early Persian converts to Islam believed strongly that the prophet's chosen leaders provided a direct line back to the prophet himself and therefore to the will of God.

WAITING FOR THE HIDDEN IMAM

The Shia believed that although he had disappeared from the world, for a time the last imam still spoke to his followers. His words reached them through leaders they called *bab,* a word that means "gate." There were four *babs* until, in the year 941, the last *bab* died without naming a successor. Believers no longer had a direct link to the Hidden Imam, but they understood that one day a messenger would appear. This One would once again provide a direct line to the divine will of God for humanity. For the next thousand years devout Persian Muslims waited for the return of the Hidden Imam.

THE TWELFTH IMAM

The line of imams lasted through 12 generations. The Twelfth Imam was only a child when he became imam. According to tradition in the year 873 (the year 260 on the Islamic calendar) the Twelfth Imam withdrew from the world and was never seen again. People believed that he would come again to lead them into a new world of justice and harmony. Over time he became known as the Hidden Imam, or the Mahdi, a title that meant "The One Who Would Arise."

In the mid-19th century many people believed that the One promised in the Quran would soon come. In Persia believers began to gather around a religious leader named Siyyid Ali Muhammad. *Siyyid* is a title of respect for descendants of the prophet Muhammad. Siyyid Ali Muhammad was descended from the prophet on both his mother's side and his father's side. His relationship to the prophet gave him credibility. To his followers Siyyid Ali Muhammad was the promised messenger of God. They believed that through him they would receive truth and enlightenment. They began to call him the Bab. They called themselves Babis, or "followers of the Bab."

Siyyid Ali Muhammad was born on October 20, 1819, in Shiraz, Persia. Ali Muhammad was very young when his father died. He had little education but he was exceptionally bright. Even as a child he impressed adults with his understanding of scripture and of spiritual matters.

At 15 he became a merchant like his father before him. By all accounts he was a good businessman. He became known not only for his business ability but also for his honesty and fairness. After several years, when he was in his early 20s, he closed his business and traveled for a year to Iraq. He visited the holy cities of Islam and met Muslim leaders. On his return to Persia in 1842 he married the daughter of another merchant. The couple's only child died as an infant the following year.

Among those who knew him Ali Muhammad became known for extreme piety and his great interest in religion. People began to remark on his holiness and some even described him as a saint. Around this time he began to have dreams in which holy figures of Islamic history appeared to him. He took these dreams as a sign that the spirit of God had come into his soul. He began to write down his thoughts on religious matters. As a rule only trained religious scholars did such writing, and Ali Muhammad had no such training. However he felt divinely inspired. At first his reputation and beliefs were limited to his locality, but gradually they spread far and wide across Persia.

THE BAB'S DECLARATION

On May 23, 1844, Siyyid Ali Muhammad announced that he was the bearer of divine truth. People attached great importance to the fact that this was the year 1260 on the Islamic calendar—exactly 1,000 years after the disappearance of the Hidden Imam. At first his followers understood him to be saying that he was the new gateway to the Hidden Imam, for whom they had been waiting. Later they interpreted his words to be a claim that he was the Mahdi himself. Either way, he set in motion a religious upheaval that was to have lasting effects.

The room in the Bab's house in Shiraz where he declared his mission on May 23, 1844.

BEGINNINGS OF THE BABI MOVEMENT

A man of great personal charm, the Bab had already begun gathering followers. One of these was a young religious stu-

dent named Mulla Husayn. Mulla Husayn's studies had led him to believe that the Promised One of the scriptures would soon arrive. When he heard from Siyyid Ali Muhammad's own lips that Siyyid Ali Muhammad was the promised one awaited by all faiths, he immediately declared his faith. Within several weeks 17 others had joined him.

Other early followers included a young man named Muhammad Ali-i-Barfurush, whom the Bab called Quddus, or "Most Holy," and a young woman with whom the Bab was corresponding, later known as Tahirih, "The Pure One." The Bab called these first 18 followers the "Letters of the Living." He told them to go throughout Persia spreading the good news that the Promised One was coming.

THE BAB'S MESSAGE

Many things about the Bab worked to convince his followers that he was a divine leader. He had a remarkable ability to explain passages from the Quran. Scholars had puzzled over these passages for centuries. Highly spiritual, the Bab had a strong effect on his listeners, who believed that his speech was divinely inspired. He revealed more than 100,000 new verses in the style and spirit of the Quran, which his followers firmly believed to have come directly from God.

Even more striking than his discussions of religious matters and spiritual revelations was his view for society. His vision was broad in scope. In his most important book, the Bayan, he wrote that a time was coming when new forms of learning and science would appear. He called on people to embrace learning and to help bring about a new society. He provided the principles for a Babi society. These included a system of laws for society to live by. They also laid down rules for matters such as marriage, divorce, and inheritance. Another section gives rules for the relationship between the Babi state and other nations. Above all the Bab's vision was a peaceful one. He rejected the idea that converts could be won by the sword. He urged his followers to be gentle and cause no sorrow to others.

Babi disciples traveled to all the cities of Persia with the good news of the Bab's coming. It was news that people had been waiting for and many accepted it eagerly.

TROUBLE FOR THE BABIS

Although the belief in the return of the Hidden Imam persisted among the Persian people, the clergy was less receptive to the idea. Indeed the actions of the Bab's followers infuriated and outraged them.

In Islam the prophet Muhammad is the final prophet. His word as recorded in the Quran is perfect in understanding and revealing God's purpose. The Bab's followers were presenting his words as the newly revealed word of God. The Shii clergy, therefore, saw the Bab's claim as heresy. Furthermore it was a threat to their power. If people accepted the Bab as the true speaker for the Hidden Imam, he would become the highest authority in Islam, and they would have to take their orders from him. The clergy immediately rose up against him.

RULINGS OF RELIGIOUS COURTS

The Shii clergy held great power in 19th-century Persia. The country's ruler, the shah, supported the rulings of their religious courts. Their decrees therefore had the force of law, which the Persian army could enforce. Clergy also used the power of the pulpit. When they preached that someone was a heretic, they could easily turn the minds of their congregations against him. It was a small step to rioting and civil unrest.

In spite of being labeled an infidel and a heretic, the Bab attracted followers across Persia. The Bab even began to attract some members of the clergy. This disturbed and angered Muslim leaders even more. Anyone who attracted followers was a threat to them. They had the Bab placed under house arrest in Shiraz. However even though the Bab's movements were restricted, his followers in distant cities were persuading more and more people of the truth of the Bab's claims. Also, people who came to visit him went away persuaded. The movement continued to grow.

WINNING HEARTS AND MINDS

One of the early converts was a man called Vahid, a religious scholar with a sharp theological mind. Vahid had connections to the court and may have been sent by the shah to find out more about this "Shirazi saint" who was attracting so much attention. The Bab converted Vahid as well. Winning members of the clergy to his side was an important step for the Bab in winning the minds and hearts of the people. The number of Babis swelled.

IMPRISONMENT AND TRIAL

In September 1846 the Bab was able to escape house arrest and leave Shiraz. He had hopes of traveling to Tehran to meet with

A cabinet containing photographs of the Bab and Baha'u'llah.

the shah. Instead the shah's prime minister had him arrested, taken to Azerbaijan, and imprisoned there. Azerbaijan, although part of Iran at the time, was far from the shah's court. The prime minister hoped that the Azerbaijanis would ignore the Bab's message. The opposite proved true. The new faith took root there. So the prime minister moved the Bab to a Kurdish area of Iran and threw him into the prison at Chihriq. This tactic too was a failure, as the Kurd leaders became admirers of the Bab.

During this time the traditional clergy continued to preach against the Bab. His followers came under increasing attacks from mobs that the clergy had aroused to violence. The mobs believed that they were waging a jihad, a Muslim holy war against unbelievers. The Bab's followers turned to him, hoping that he would bless their own fight against the people who were persecuting them. The Bab, however, rejected the notion of a counter-jihad. Babis could defend themselves if their lives were threatened, but they were otherwise not to fight on behalf of the faith. The survival of the faith, the Bab decreed, was in the hands of God.

"THE PURE ONE"

One of the converts was a woman known as Tahirih, "The Pure One," who attracted attention and became one of the most remarkable leaders of the Babi movement. Encouraged by a family of scholars, Tahirih was able to study the Quran with her brothers in a time when few women learned to read or write. She mastered its ideas easily, and also became a gifted poet. The young woman was much taken with the Bab's ideas and began corresponding with him. He quickly named her one of the Letters of the Living. She never met the Bab face to face, but their vigorous correspondence made her an important teacher of the emerging faith.

THE CONFERENCE AT BADASHT

With the Bab in prison leaders of the Babi Faith met in the village of Badasht to the northeast of Tehran. One of their goals was to come up with a plan to free the Bab. Another was to share their understanding of the Bab's teachings so they could go on leading in his absence. Among the leaders of the conference was the woman poet Tahirih. She electrified the conference when she announced that the Bab was not just a reformer; he was the Imam Mahdi, the Promised One. She went on to say that this meant that Babis were no longer bound by the requirements of Muslim law. As followers of the Bab they must look to him for guidance.

She began by casting off her veil and head covering. Her action caused an immediate stir. Many of the more conservative Babis were shocked. They had never seen a woman unveiled in public. Even more, it caused the Muslim clerics to brand the Babis as atheists and their women as immodest and impure. However the Bab's doctrines clearly indicated that women were equal participants with men in the new religion.

BABIS UNDER SIEGE

The shah of Persia died in 1848, throwing the country into a state of political unrest. The Babis found themselves under even greater pressure from the Muslim clergy, who were trying to stamp them out. A group of Babis under Mulla Husayn had been traveling around the country proclaiming the Bab as the Promised One. They called on the people to follow him. The Shii clergy preached vigorously from the pulpit that they were heretics. Rioting followed. The Babis withdrew to the shrine of a Muslim saint, Shaykh Tabarsi, and hoped it would be a safe place. They quickly put up a fort for protection.

However their troubles were not over. The clergy accused them of causing the riots. This time the government decided that the Babi movement must be wiped out. Officials sent a band of armed soldiers to add to the clergy and rioters already crying for Babi blood.

THE SIEGE AT SHAYKH TABARSI

Over the next year more and more troops came and attacked the fort. They built a series of barricades around it, so the Babis

THE BAB IS PUNISHED

Muslim clergy called for the Bab to be tried before a panel of religious scholars. In the summer of 1848 the trial took place. The Bab was sentenced to a cruel and painful form of physical punishment, the bastinado, in which the soles of his feet were beaten with sticks. During this torture one of the men beating the Bab accidentally struck him in the face. The leaders called for a doctor. Dr. William Cormick, an Englishman, responded. He was deeply impressed with the Bab, whom he found to be mild and uncomplaining.

(He) was a very mild and delicate-looking man, rather small in stature and very fair for a Persian, with a melodious soft voice, which struck me much . . . In fact his whole look and deportment went far to dispose one in his favor . . .

(From the memoirs of Dr. William Cormick.)

were effectively trapped inside. Led by Mulla Husayn, the Babis had been able to beat back their attackers for a time. However eventually a few hundred Babis inside the fort were defending themselves against a large army, which was camped outside. The Babis were also running out of water. They managed to dig a well but it was clear that their situation was becoming desperate. Mulla Husayn decided to charge the barricades. He knew he would probably die. He called on his companions "to partake of the cup of martyrdom" with him.

That day Mulla Husayn bathed in the water from the well, dressed in clean clothes, and prepared himself for battle. Before dawn he led his band of Babi fighters out of the fort. They broke through first one and then another set of barricades until they were finally outside. However their success was costly and short-lived. A sniper who had climbed a tree shot Mulla Husayn in the chest. His companions carried him back to the fort, where he died a few hours later.

THE END OF THE SIEGE

At last the remaining Babis gave up the struggle and agreed to surrender. The army swore on the Quran that the Babis would be permitted to leave safely. However as soon as they left the fort the army set on them again. Those who were not killed outright were tortured to death or sold into slavery.

The Bab's Final Statement

Oh wayward generation! Had you believed in me every one of you would have followed the example of this youth, who stood in rank above most of you, and would have willingly sacrificed himself in my path. The day will come when you will have recognized me; that day I shall have ceased to be with you.

This horrible scene played itself out in other towns as well. In Nayriz in the south of Persia and in Zanjan in the northwest the Shii clergy aroused their followers to riot and then blamed the Babis. The government's troops joined in. People hunted the Babis down, seized their property, and killed them.

Vahid, another respected Babi leader, died at Nayriz. At Zanjan, as at Shaykh Tabarsi, officials offered a pledge of peace signed on the Quran. As soon as the Babis came out they were slaughtered. A large number of Babis were arrested and publicly executed when they refused to reject their new faith. A few, however, survived to tell what had happened.

THE DEATH OF THE BAB

While all of this unrest was going on the prime minister ordered the Bab's execution. The Bab had done nothing that was against civil law, however. So the prime minister had the Bab taken to Tabriz, a city in northwestern Iran, where the clergy signed the death sentence for a crime against Islam.

Eyewitness accounts record the remarkable events surrounding the execution of the Bab. The army jailers suspended the Bab and one of his young followers by ropes from the top of a wall. A firing squad of 750 Armenian Christian soldiers lined up facing them. The order to fire was given. The rifles made a deafening roar and black smoke filled the entire area. When the smoke cleared the Bab's companion stood by the wall, unhurt. The Bab had disappeared.

Searchers found him in his room calmly dictating to his secretary. The original firing squad was so shaken by what had happened that they refused to continue. Many believed that they had attempted to kill a holy man and now feared the wrath of God. Officials quickly brought together a squad of Muslim marksmen to carry out the execution. This time the soldiers did not miss and the Bab was killed.

The story of the Bab's death spread throughout Persia like the wind. It had a profound impact not only on the Persian people but also on the many Europeans who lived in Persia at the time. It aroused new interest in his message—not just within his native country but also from the outside world.

A Western Reaction to the Bab's Martyrdom

This is one of the most magnificent examples of courage which mankind has ever been able to witness, and it is also an admirable proof of the love which our hero had for his fellow countrymen. He sacrificed himself for mankind; he gave for it his body and his soul, he suffered for it hardships, insults, indignities, torture and martyrdom. He sealed with his blood the pact of universal brotherhood, and like Jesus he gave his life in order to herald the reign of concord, justice, and love for one's fellow men.

(A. L. M. Nicholas, a French consular official, 1850.)

THE COLLAPSE OF BABISM

For the surviving Babis, however, the Bab's death was a disaster. In a few months they had lost not only the Bab but also most of the Letters of the Living. Mulla Husayn had died in the siege at Shaykh Tabarsi, and Vahid at Nayriz. Quddus, the gentle young man and Letter of the Living whom the Bab called "Most Holy," was dragged through the streets in chains and finally tortured to death.

In despair two young Babis attempted to kill the shah. They did not seriously harm him but the attempt aroused a new wave of violence against people who had done nothing but declare their faith in a man of peace and love. Babis were rounded up and tortured in unimaginable ways. Tahirih, the Pure One, although she had not been involved in the plot to kill the shah, was put to death. Defiant to the end,

The shrine of Mirza Husayn Ali Nuri , or Baha'u'llah, in Akko, Israel, as photographed around 1910. Baha'u'llah established the Baha'i Faith following the death of the Bab.

she is said to have looked her executioners in the eye and said, "You can kill me as soon as you like, but you cannot stop the emancipation of women."

The massacre of several thousand of the Bab's followers, and the Bab's own death, left the Babis leaderless and disorganized. By 1852 it appeared that the new faith, begun in such hope, would vanish in complete failure.

The Bab's followers had found in him a messenger of God in the line of Moses, Jesus, and Muhammad, all founders and leaders of great religions. However his writings showed that the Bab did not see himself as the final prophet. The door was open for yet another leader—"He Whom God Will Make Manifest." The spiritual needs that had led people to follow the Bab remained strong. The seeds of a new religion had been planted, and in time they would grow again with renewed strength as the Baha'i Faith.

The Death of Quddus

. . . how, barefooted, bareheaded, and loaded with chains, he was paraded through the streets, followed and scorned by the entire population of the town; how he was execrated and spat upon by the howling mob; how he was assailed with the knives and axes of the scum of its female inhabitants; how his body was pierced and mutilated, and how eventually it was delivered to the flames!

Amidst his torments, Quddus was heard whispering forgiveness to his foes. "Forgive, O my God," he cried, "the trespasses of this people. Deal with them in Thy mercy, for they know not what we already have discovered and cherish".

(In Nabil, *The Dawn-Breakers*, translated by Shoghi Effendi.)

CHAPTER 3

BAHA'U'LLAH, FOUNDER OF THE BAHA'I FAITH

One important follower of the Bab escaped the fatal end of so many others. His name was Mirza Husayn Ali Nuri. Mirza Husayn Ali Nuri was born on November 12, 1817, in Tehran, Persia (now Iran). His family was Persian nobility. His father was a landowner and a government official. The family was well-to-do and socially prominent, and the boy's father held a high position in the Persian court. Young Mirza Husayn Ali had no formal education; he was homeschooled. He read widely, however, and learned quickly. From an early age he was devoutly religious.

Mirza Husayn Ali was 22 years old when his father died. Although he was young, officials offered him his father's government position; he turned it down. He preferred instead to stay at home, managing the family property and looking after the education of his younger family members. He also donated time and money to many charities in the region. In spite of his youth he quickly came to be called "Father of the Poor" by the people in the region where he lived. He also gained a reputation for integrity and honesty at a time when many wealthy and important people were corrupt and dishonest.

Path leading to the shrine of Baha'u'llah at Bhaji, outside Akko (formerly Acre), Israel. This is considered the most holy place in the Baha'i world.

MIRZA HUSAYN ALI CONVERTS TO BABISM

In 1844 Mirza Husayn Ali received a visit from Mulla Husayn, one of the Bab's early disciples. At the age of 27 Mirza Husayn Ali was already known for his good works and religious devotion. The Bab sent Mulla Husayn to Tehran to deliver a letter to Mirza Husayn Ali. As a result of receiving that letter Mirza Husayn Ali became a follower of the Bab, along with four of his brothers and half brothers. His conversion was important to the Bab and to the Babi movement. Most early converts were religious students like Mulla Husayn, or came from merchant or peasant classes. Mirza Husayn Ali's family were landowners with ties to the government. They were an important addition to the Babi cause.

PREACHING THE MESSAGE OF THE BAB

From the time of his conversion onward, Mirza Husayn Ali Nuri worked energetically at spreading the Babi Faith. He traveled across Persia to preach the Bab's message. Because of his wealth and high social standing he had access to others in his social class, and he converted a significant number of people, including other members of his own family. He used his personal wealth to finance the teaching of Babism in other regions. His social position also helped to protect him from the persecution that Babi followers were beginning to experience.

Soon after Mirza Husayn Ali became a Babi he began writing letters to the Bab, who was then imprisoned in Chihriq prison. The Bab responded with letters of his own, and Mirza Husayn Ali gained an impressive knowledge of the Bab's thinking and outlook. Other Babi leaders such as Vahid, Quddus, Mulla Husayn, and Tahirih drew him into their inner circle.

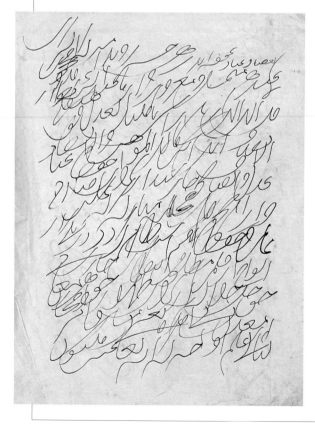

One of the many letters dictated by Baha'u'llah to his secretary. Baha'u'llah would dictate so quickly that his secretary could barely keep up with the flow of his words.

They began to look upon Mirza Husayn Ali as an important interpreter of the Bab's teachings.

BAHA'U'LLAH—"GLORY OF GOD"

In 1848 Mirza Husayn Ali organized and helped to direct the gathering of Babis in the village of Badasht; this conference at Badasht gave Babism a new and more revolutionary direction. It was also at the Badasht Conference that Mirza Husayn Ali gave each of the Babis gathered there a new name, one that reflected their spiritual qualities. For himself he chose the name Baha, which means "Splendor" or "Glory."

After the conference the Bab wrote to each of the participants using the new name that Mirza Husayn Ali had given them. To the newly named Baha the Bab sent a rare and wonderful work of calligraphy, or handwriting, that he had done himself, in the shape of a star. It included the title Baha'u'llah, or "Glory of God," the name by which Mirza Husayn Ali Nuri soon came to be known among his followers.

Map showing the route of Baha'u'llah's exile. The regions and place names are those of the time.

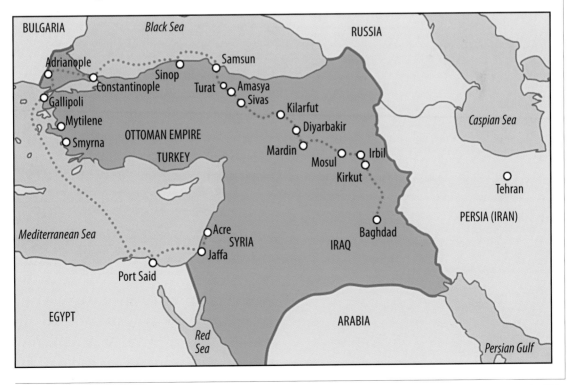

HE WHOM GOD WILL MAKE MANIFEST

As Baha'u'llah lay in chains in the dungeon he heard a voice speaking to him. The voice, which seemed to come from all sides, said:

Verily (truly) we shall render thee victorious by thyself and by thy pen. Grieve thou not for that which has befallen thee, neither be thou afraid, for thou art in safety. Ere long will God raise up the treasures of the earth—men who will aid thee through thyself and thy name, wherewith God hath revived the hearts of such as have recognized him . . .

In spite of the filth and suffering that surrounded him Baha'u'llah felt new power and strength. He understood that he was the person whom the Bab had promised, the one who was ordained by God to lead his people into a new understanding and faith.

Carved seals used to stamp letters verifying Baha'u'llah as the author of written papers. Baha'u'llah wrote thousands of letters teaching, advising, and supporting the Baha'i community.

PERSECUTION INCREASES

The conference at Badasht drew attention to the Babis. The new movement was growing so fast that it became a threat to the existing order. Its members came under attack. It was at this time that officials arrested Tahirih and threw her into jail. Baha'u'llah tried to help her, but was himself imprisoned and tortured by having the soles of his feet beaten with bamboo rods.

Free again, Baha'u'llah tried to convince his friends in the government that the Babis were peace-loving and would do no harm. In turn his friends tried to persuade him to stop his work on behalf of the Bab, but he refused. He warned them that if the attacks did not stop there would be trouble.

The attacks against the Babis continued, and trouble did indeed follow with the attempt on the shah's life in 1852. Feelings against the Babis were now so strong that Baha'u'llah's connections to government and power could no longer help him. He was arrested again, and taken to Tehran, where he was locked up for four months in a prison so foul and terrible that it was known as the Siyah-Chal, or "Black Pit." Deep underground, cold, dark, and damp, it had once been a reservoir for one of Tehran's public baths. As Baha'u'llah described it, "The dungeon was wrapped in thick darkness, and our fellow prisoners numbered nearly a hundred and fifty souls: thieves, assassins, and highwaymen

A view of the city of Tehran, where Baha'u'llah was imprisoned in 1852. The photograph was taken in 1930, but the city would have looked very similar 80 years earlier.

. . . Most of these men had neither clothes nor bedding to lie on. God alone knoweth what befell us in that most foul-smelling and gloomy place!" It was here that Baha'u'llah realized he was destined to become a spiritual leader.

All over Persia Babis were being persecuted and attacked. The Babi prisoners in the Siyah-Chal were chained together so they could hardly move. The stench was so awful that they could barely breathe. They were under constant threat of torture and death. Each day their jailers descended into the pit, chose one man, and executed him.

BANISHMENT

Somehow Baha'u'llah survived his imprisonment. Because of his family's influence, officials knew that they could not execute him without a trial. They also knew he had done no wrong and there was no evidence against him. Their hesitancy was also partly due to the vigorous protests against the Babi massacres registered by both the Russian and British embassies.

However officials were reluctant to let Baha'u'llah go. They knew that he would immediately attract followers to the Bab's cause. Finally the prime minister, who was a relative of Baha'u'llah, persuaded the court that Baha'u'llah should be banished from Persia. As part of his banishment the government confiscated his property. They destroyed or seized all his books and works of art. They looted and burned his home. His possessions and property gone, still suffering from the beatings he had received, and weak from his four months in prison, he was released without a trial in 1852.

Baha'u'llah came out of prison weaker in body but even stronger in spirit than when he was arrested. Under the conditions of

A father and his son (left) and members of the Baha'i community in chains after being arrested. This photograph was taken around 1896. The founders and members of the Baha'i Faith endured many years of persecution and banishment for their beliefs.

his release from prison, Baha'u'llah had to leave Persia. He no longer had any possessions, but his family and followers could go with him if they wished. In 1852 chose to go to Baghdad in Iraq.

At first Baha'u'llah said nothing about the voice he had heard and its message. He settled in Baghdad and lived quietly with his family. Over the next three years other Babis joined him and formed a small community.

MIRZA YAHYA

One member of the community was Baha'u'llah's half brother, Mirza Yahya, or Subh-i-Azal. He was 13 years younger than Baha'u'llah and had followed him into the Babi Faith. After the

conference at Badasht the Bab had named Mirza Yahya as the one to be the head of the Babi Faith if the Bab were to die. At the time the Bab was in prison, and he and Baha'u'llah both felt that Baha'u'llah could do the most good for the faith from behind the scenes. Since Baha'u'llah was both older and wiser than his brother, they believed that Mirza Yahya would continue to take his advice.

Mirza Yahya was easily swayed. After the Bab's death he fell under the influence of a Muslim cleric named Siyyid Muhammad. Siyyid Muhammad reminded Yahya that the Bab had chosen him, not Baha'u'llah. He persuaded Yahya to renounce his brother and proclaim himself the Babi authority.

Baha'u'llah realized that if he were to fight with his brother over the leadership of the community, the community would be weakened even further. He withdrew to the mountains, where he remained alone for two years. He later wrote of this time:

"Alone, we communed with Our spirit, oblivious of the world and all that is therein." Baha'u'llah spent the time fruitfully by meditating and writing.

BAHA'U'LLAH RETURNS

Meanwhile the Babi community in Baghdad was going through difficult times. Mirza Yahya proved to be a poor leader. Moreover, he could not answer theological questions as his brother had done. Would-be leaders fought for power, throwing the community into turmoil.

Faithful Babis began searching for Baha'u'llah. Finally they found him in his mountain hideaway and persuaded him to return with them. By that time things were so bad that even Mirza Yahya joined in calling for Baha'u'llah's return. Baha'u'llah returned to Baghdad in March 1856 and assumed control over the Babi community there.

During the next seven years Babism experienced a rebirth. Baha'u'llah's reputation as a spiritual leader spread, and he attracted many new followers. He composed the Kitab-i-Iqan, or "Book of Certitude," which describes God's plan for humanity and explains Baha'u'llah's mission.

Baha'u'llah's growing reputation did not please everyone. Back in Persia the shah once again felt that his power and authority were being threatened. He persuaded the government in Baghdad to move Baha'u'llah and his group farther away from the Persian border. This time they chose to move the group to Constantinople, which is now Istanbul, Turkey.

THE RIDVAN DECLARATION

Before moving to Constantinople Baha'u'llah went to stay on an island in the Tigris River. In a garden there, which he called the Garden of Ridvan (Paradise), he gathered his closest followers around him and told them of the revelation he had received in prison. He was, he explained, "He Whom God Will Make Manifest," the divine messenger that the Bab and the scriptures of other religions had promised. Today Baha'is worldwide celebrate the Ridvan Festival, as it is called, for 12 days every year, from April 21 to May 2.

For the time being, however, Baha'u'llah's followers kept his revelation a secret among themselves. The group arrived in Constantinople in August, but they were not permitted to stay long. Constantinople was the capital of the Ottoman Empire, which was experiencing unrest. Playing on the fears of the Ottoman rulers, the Persian shah represented the Babis as a threat. He pressed to have them moved again. Wanting no more trouble, the Turks agreed. So in December 1863, Baha'u'llah, his family, and his companions were sent to Adrianople (now Edirne) in European Turkey, still farther from Persian borders.

A NEW RELIGION ARISES

If the shah had hoped to silence Baha'u'llah, he failed. Visitors from all over Persia continued to flock to wherever Baha'u'llah settled. The widely scattered Babi followers knew that Baha'u'llah had drawn the Baghdad community back together when it was

The sea gate where Baha'u'llah and his companions entered Acre. On August 21, 1868, Baha'u'llah, his family, and his followers were rounded up in Adrianople (now Edirne) in western Turkey. They were put on a boat to be taken to prison in Acre, Palestine (now Akko, Israel).

on the verge of collapse. They turned to him as their spiritual leader. Baha'u'llah decided that it was time to announce his revelation to all the Babis.

Mirza Yahya was still the official head of the Babi Faith. Although he had wanted Baha'u'llah to come back to Baghdad and help him out when things were bad, he had never fully accepted his own loss of status. When the group moved to Adrianople, Mirza Yahya, still under the influence of Siyyid Muhammad, began plotting to get his power back. When this failed he twice tried to have Baha'u'llah killed, but the attempts failed.

Baha'u'llah in turn sent Mirza Yahya an announcement in which he pressed his claim to be He Whom God Will Make Manifest and asked for Mirza Yahya's support. Instead Mirza Yahya claimed that he, rather than Baha'u'llah, was the one whose coming the Bab had promised. Instead of the results Mirza Yahya wanted, however, his announcement clarified the differences between him and his brother and showed who was the true leader. Almost all the Babis deserted Mirza Yahya and accepted Baha'u'llah as the head of the faith.

The followers of Baha'u'llah now began to describe themselves as Baha'is, and the Baha'i Faith began to emerge as a separate religion.

THE PROCLAMATION OF BAHA'U'LLAH

The former followers of the Bab had accepted Baha'u'llah as their unquestioned leader. He now needed to establish himself and the new religion on the world stage. In 1867 he began writing letters to world political and religious leaders. In these let-

Shoghi Effendi's Summary of Baha'u'llah's Achievement

God's new-born Faith, the cynosure of all past Dispensations, had been fully and unreservedly proclaimed. The prophecies announcing its advent had been remarkably fulfilled. Its fundamental laws and cardinal principles, the warp and woof of the fabric of its future World Order, had been clearly enunciated. Its organic relation to, and its attitude towards, the religious systems which preceded it had been unmistakably defined. The primary institutions, within which an embryonic World Order was destined to mature, had been unassailably established. The Covenant designed to safeguard the unity and integrity of its world-embracing system had been irrevocably bequeathed to posterity. The promise of the unification of the whole human race, of the inauguration of the Most Great Peace, of the unfoldment of a world civilization, had been incontestably given.

(In Shoghi Effendi, *God Passes By*.)

ters he proclaimed himself to be the One whose return had been promised in the Torah, the New Testament, and the Quran.

Baha'u'llah told of the coming of a new world order. Its outcome would be a world civilization that recognized the oneness of the human race. "The earth," he wrote, "is but one country, and mankind its citizens." He explained that governments were meant to serve the causes of international peace, social justice, and world unity. Governments that did not work for these goals would bring disaster on themselves.

In many parts of the world Baha'u'llah's letters had little effect. However in Iran, where the shah felt insecure in his seat of power, they set off a strong reaction. Mirza Yahya, still angry from his loss of prestige and power in the Babi community, saw the letters as a way to play on the shah's fears. He and others such as Siyyid Muhammad wrote letters accusing Baha'u'llah of trying to overthrow the Ottoman government in Constantinople, which was already weak from years of fighting. The Persian ambassador

On their way to their imprisonment in Acre, Baha'u'llah and a group of 80 followers, including his family, spent three nights in Gallipoli on the Turkish coast.

to Constantinople pointed to the letters as proof. He pointed to the steady stream of visitors that Baha'u'llah attracted and hinted that these people were conspiring against the shah. Finally the ruler in Constantinople ordered that the group in Adrianople be imprisoned in the fortress at Acre.

The interior of the prison in Acre (Akko) in which Baha'u'llah and his family were kept.

On August 21, 1868, soldiers rounded up Baha'u'llah and his family and followers, about 80 total, and put them on a boat to Acre. After a miserable 10 days on a stormy Mediterranean Sea they reached land and were taken to prison under heavy guard. Ironically one of those deported to Acre along with Baha'u'llah was Siyyid Muhammad, who had plotted against him.

IMPRISONMENT AT ACRE

The penal colony at Acre was a grim and terrible place. It was a prison city where the worst criminals from all over the Ottoman Empire were sent. It lay on the shores of the Mediterranean Sea and was constantly awash in its tides. Its buildings were damp and crumbling; rotting refuse washed into it. The officials who sent Baha'u'llah there frankly hoped he would not survive. A number of the group did die, including Baha'u'llah's second son.

A small group of Babis remained loyal to Yahya and called themselves Azalis. They continued to harass the Baha'is and they tried to convince the Ottoman authorities that the Baha'is were plotting against them. A group of angry Baha'is finally rose up and killed their tormentors, an event that caused Baha'u'llah great distress. He rejected all violence no matter what the circumstances. Its use by his followers brought him deep and long-lasting grief.

THE LAST YEARS OF BAHA'U'LLAH

By 1877 prison officials were no longer bothering to enforce the orders that had kept the Baha'is behind bars. Baha'u'llah was free to come and go. He moved to a mansion his followers bought for him at Bahji, outside the city. There he lived quietly, writing, meditating, and enjoying his gardens.

MOST HOLY BOOK

In spite of the dreadful conditions Baha'u'llah continued to preach goodness and to live according to his beliefs. He lived in the Acre prison for nine years, first inside the prison walls and then under house arrest within the city of Acre. Nevertheless he managed to establish contact with the Baha'is in Iran. And it was at this time that he also wrote one of the great works of Baha'i scripture, the Kitab-i-Aqdas, or Most Holy Book. Gradually his profound goodness and faith began to win over his jailers, and the prisoners' situation improved.

A Subject of Devotion and Love

While living at Bahji Baha'u'llah received visitors from the many places to which the Baha'i Faith had begun to spread. One visitor was an English scholar, Edward Granville Browne, whom Baha'u'llah impressed deeply. Browne wrote:

No need to ask in whose presence I stood. I bowed myself before the one who is the object of a devotion and love which kings might envy and emperors sigh for in vain . . . Those piercing eyes seemed to read one's very soul; power and authority sat on that ample brow; while the deep lines on the forehead and face implied an age which the jet-black hair and beard flowing down in indistinguishable luxuriance almost to the waist seemed to belie . . .

(In Moojan Momen, *A Short Introduction to the Baha'i Faith*.)

Baha'u'llah lived until 1892. He died at the age of 74. For more than 40 years of his life he had been a prisoner and an exile from his home. Born to luxury and wealth, he experienced poverty, hunger, grief, injustice, and suffering firsthand. He had been chained and beaten. He had even watched his children die in the brutal conditions of imprisonment. The religion that began with him reflects his deep identification with the poor and the suffering of the world.

During Baha'u'llah's last years the young Baha'i Faith continued to spread. It now reached into Egypt, Russia, Turkey,

The entrance to the door of the shrine where Baha'u'llah is buried in Haifa, Israel.

KEY DATES IN THE LIFE OF BAHA'U'LLAH

1817 Born November 12

1844 Converts to Babism

1848 Attends conference at Badasht

1852 Imprisoned at Siyah-Chal; receives revelation from God freed from prison; banished to Baghdad

1854 Withdraws to the mountains

1856 Returns to Baghdad, takes control of Babi community completes Hidden Words

1862 Completes Kitab-i-Iqan ("Book of Certitude")

1863 Banished to Constantinople, makes Ridvan Declaration; banished to Adrianople (Edirne)

1868 Imprisoned in Acre (Akko)

1873 Completes Kitab-i-Aqdas ("Most Holy Book")

1877 Allowed to leave Acre

1879 Moves to Bahji

1892 Dies May 29

Central Asia, and even India. It continued to grow in Persia, its birthplace. In spite of everything that governments and a powerful clergy could throw at it—persecution, angry mobs, and official injustice—it would not be stamped out.

In his will Baha'u'llah named his oldest surviving son, 'Abdu'l-Baha, to be leader of the faith after him. He also left instructions for taking the developing religion into the 20th century, which was fast approaching.

CHAPTER 4

THE BAHA'I SCRIPTURES

The Baha'i scriptures include the writings of the faith's three central figures: Baha'u'llah, his son 'Abdu'l-Baha, and the Bab.

THE WRITINGS OF BAHA'U'LLAH

For Baha'i believers the writings of Baha'u'llah are the divine word of God. Baha'u'llah's books include Kalimat-i-Maknunih (which means "The Hidden Words," written around 1858); Kitab-i-Iqan, ("The Book of Certitude," 1862); and Kitab-i-Aqdas ("Most Holy Book," 1873). He also wrote many "tablets" or letters. He himself estimated that a collection of his letters would make over 100 volumes. All of these works and others convey Baha'u'llah's message and lay down rules for leading the Baha'i life.

One important source of scripture for the Baha'i Faith is *Gleanings from the Writings of Baha'u'llah*. This is a collection of Baha'ullah's writings. It was compiled and translated into English by his great-grandson, Shoghi Effendi. From the more than 15,000 tablets Baha'u'llah produced in his lifetime Shoghi Effendi chose passages that he felt would show the spirit of Baha'i teachings.

The International Baha'i Archives in Haifa, Israel was built by Shoghi Effendi to house important Baha'i relics and scriptures associated with the lives of the Bab, Baha'u'llah and 'Abdu'l-Baha.

THE TRANSLATIONS

Shoghi Effendi was Baha'u'llah's principal translator. He spoke fluent English as well as Persian and Arabic. After 'Abdu'l-Baha's death, Shoghi Effendi became Guardian of the Faith, as his grandfather's will stated. As Guardian, he was the only person with the authority to interpret Baha'u'llah's message.

It was Shoghi Effendi who set the style for the Baha'i scriptures. He chose a formal and older style of writing as he believed this style more closely reflected the stately Persian and Arabic that Baha'u'llah used. Shoghi Effendi also chose to use the word *mankind* to refer to all humanity and the masculine pronouns *he* and *him* to refer to God. He may have done so because the masculine form was considered the proper formal usage in written English when he was writing. Baha'u'llah's teachings specifically do not attach any gender to the creator. Baha'i readers understand and accept that words like *men* and *mankind* refer to all humanity, not just men.

Shoghi Effendi's translations into English are the highest authority for interpreting Baha'u'llah's writings. Translators use them, not the original Persian or Arabic works, when they translate Baha'u'llah's writings into other languages.

THE TEACHINGS OF BAHA'U'LLAH

Baha'u'llah's message reaches the whole world. His vision is of a global religion that embraces all peoples of the earth. All people, whatever their country of origin, their race, or their ethnic background, are basically the same. Baha'u'llah recognizes only one race—the human race. He asks his followers to act in the best interests of all humankind. There are Baha'i communities on all continents and the Baha'i scriptures have been translated into 802 languages.

THE HIDDEN WORDS

In the Kalimat-i-Maknunih, or Hidden Words, Baha'u'llah restates the essential spiritual truths and ethical teachings that founders of all world religions have taught. The Hidden Words is quite short. It has only 52 pages. There are two sections: Words from the Arabic, with 71 numbered passages, and Words from the Persian, with 82 passages. Each passage is only a few lines long. As in the scriptures of other faiths, the passages take the form of the voice of God speaking to the reader.

In the Arabic Hidden Words, God advises his children. "My first counsel is this: Possess a pure, kindly and radiant heart." His words urge believers to love him and only him. The words also remind human beings of the great love God has for them.

The Persian Hidden Words carry a similar message. In this section Baha'u'llah often uses metaphors of nature. He compares the word of God to seeds of divine wisdom and asks believers to let these words grow in their hearts. In this way beautiful flowers of knowledge and wisdom will grow in the hearts of humankind.

THE BOOK OF CERTITUDE

The Kitab-i-Iqan, or Book of Certitude, presents one of the most important themes of Baha'u'llah's teachings. This is the theme of the progressive nature of religion. Many Baha'i scriptures enlarge on this teaching. The book also deals with great religious questions such as the nature of God, the nature of humanity, and the purpose of life.

REVELATION OF GOD'S WILL

According to the message of the Iqan there is one eternal God, the creator. The essence of God is unknowable. However, throughout time God has revealed God's will and purpose for humanity through a chosen individual or messenger. Each messenger has founded a great religion. For example, through Abraham the Jews came to understand the oneness of God. Moses revealed God's law in the Ten Commandments. Jesus taught the love of God and the love of humankind. Each messenger has perfectly reflected the energy and power of God that is God's love.

A SHARED PURPOSE

According to Baha'u'llah every divine messenger has come at a time that was right for a particular point in history. Although they have appeared in different times and places, they had a shared purpose. Each

> **The Message**
>
> *My first counsel is this: Possess a pure, kindly and radiant heart, that thine may be a sovereignty ancient, imperishable, and everlasting.*
>
> (In Baha'u'llah, *The Hidden Words of Baha'u'llah*, Part I, 1.)

of these chosen leaders was right for his time and place and led people to a new understanding of God's will for humanity.

Many people have believed that the messenger of God will return, yet each messenger of God has been rejected in his time. All have undergone hardship and suffering. Baha'u'llah points out that many prophets of God have had to suffer because of what they preached. Jesus suffered and died on the cross. The prophet Muhammad of Islam cried, "No prophet of God hath suffered such harm as I have suffered." To the messengers such as Moses, Jesus, and Muhammad, Baha'u'llah adds the Bab, who died for his teachings. Such persecutions have led people of their own time to doubt that the messengers were from God. Yet throughout history people believed that they were.

How the Words of Baha'u'llah Were Recorded

From a contemporary account:

Mirza Aqa Jan [Baha'u'llah's secretary] had a large ink-pot the size of a small bowl. He also had available about ten to twelve pens and large sheets of paper in stacks . . . He would bring [letters] into the presence of Baha'u'llah and, having obtained permission, would read them. Afterwards [Baha'u'llah] would direct him to take up his pen . . .

Such was the speed with which he used to write the revealed Word that the ink of the first word was scarcely yet dry when the whole page was finished. It seemed as if someone had dipped a lock of hair in the ink and applied it over the whole page . .

Then the letters were transcribed and approved by Baha'u'llah.

TIME FOR A NEW MESSENGER

In the Iqan Baha'u'llah writes that 1,280 years have passed since the last messenger, the prophet Muhammad, offered his teachings. The time for a new messenger has come. He sees in people a yearning for the truth and the need for a new leader.

The spiritual aspects of the human relationship to God do not change. However, the conditions of life change from age to age. As time moves on God sends new messengers with lessons that are appropriate to each new age. In this way religion evolves, moving forward with time.

THE MOST HOLY BOOK

The Kitab-i-Aqdas is Baha'u'llah's book of holy law. He produced it during his prison years in Acre, probably the darkest and most difficult time of his life. For Baha'is it is his most important work. The Aqdas lays out the rules for building a new world

In November 1992 more than 27,000 Baha'is from some 170 countries assembled in New York City for the Second Baha'i World Congress. The Baha'i Faith that began in Iran in the middle of the 19th century has now spread to 236 countries and territories throughout the world.

order in which all humanity will come together under the law of God. It names and describes the institutions that will make the new world order possible. It is the guidebook for the future world society that Baha'u'llah came to establish. The main part of the Aqdas is only 190 paragraphs long, yet it covers many topics.

RELIGIOUS OBLIGATIONS

The Aqdas commands humanity to recognize Baha'u'llah as the messenger of God for this time and to obey the laws that God has given. The laws are designed to further the cause of bringing together the whole world under the Baha'i Faith.

From earlier religions Baha'u'llah retains practices such as fasting and prayer that serve a spiritual purpose. He provides specific rules for prayer, including washing the hands and face before praying, the times when prayers are to be said, and which prayers are obligatory. He forbids congregational prayer, except for the dead.

SOCIAL LAWS

Social laws cover marriage, divorce, and inheritance. The Aqdas establishes the *huququ'llah,* the voluntary wealth tax that all Baha'is pay to the faith. Baha'u'llah calls this tax "the Right of God." It supports the work of the faith.

Like the Ten Commandments of the Jewish Torah, the Aqdas forbids killing, stealing, lying, and adultery. In addition it prohibits arson, gambling, alcoholic beverages, drug abuse, and gossip; his followers are not permitted to talk about people behind their backs. Other prohibited activities are laziness, striking or wounding anyone, and creating conflict. Baha'is are to repent of their sins, but the mostly Christian practice of confession to another is prohibited. Baha'u'llah says, "(L)et repentance be between yourselves and God."

The Baha'i Calendar

Baha'u'llah establishes the Baha'i calendar and its holy days and makes fasting obligatory during the 19-day month before the New Year. However, he creates exemptions from the fast for people who are ill, children, old people, pregnant and nursing women, and those doing heavy labor.

RULES FOR LIVING THE BAHA'I LIFE

The Aqdas exhorts believers to welcome followers of all religions in fellowship. They are to honor their parents, to study and to teach the faith, and not to wish for others what they would not wish for themselves. Parents are to educate their children in reading and writing and especially in the rules of the Baha'i Faith.

Each individual is to have a trade or a craft. People are to use their skills in a way that will profit both themselves and others. They are not to be lazy or idle. Work is considered a form of worship. Baha'is are to care for their health and to be personally clean. They are to bathe regularly and to wear only clean clothes.

THE INSTITUTIONS OF THE BAHA'I FAITH

In the Aqdas Baha'u'llah also sets down practical rules for the internal structure of the Baha'i Faith. He describes the establishment of Houses of Justice in each city and a worldwide Universal

Student assembly at the City Montessori School in India. The school teaches the essential principles of all religions to children from preschool to college. The school stresses academic excellence, globalism, and interfaith harmony.

SOME RULES FOR LIVING THE BAHA'I LIFE

To be truthful
To be trustworthy
To be faithful
To be righteous and fear God
To be just and fair
To be tactful and wise
To be courteous
To be hospitable
To be persevering
To be detached
To be absolutely submissive to the will of God
Not to stir up mischief
Not to be hypocritical
Not to be proud
Not to be fanatical
Not to prefer one's self to one's neighbor
Not to contend with one's neighbor
Not to indulge one's passions
Not to lament in adversity
Not to contend with those in authority
Not to lose one's temper
Not to anger one's neighbor

House of Justice that would rule on matters of faith not specifically addressed in Baha'i scriptures. He describes the institution of guardianship to lead the faith after him. The Aqdas thus anticipated many of the institutions that the young religion would need as it grew and spread under new leadership.

THE MESSAGE OF THE AQDAS

The Aqdas is the guide for the new world order that Baha'u'llah has come to establish: If humanity will follow its commandments the world will be united as one country; war, famine, and suffering will end; and peace will rule the earth. The laws of the Aqdas are not Baha'u'llah's but God's. Baha'u'llah calls these laws "the Counsel of God"; they are God's word, God's bounty, and God's treasure for those who will listen and take them to heart. Baha'u'llah writes that the Aqdas is the beginning of divine knowledge, the lamp that will lead all the people of the human race in the path of truth.

SUPPLEMENTARY TEXTS

The Aqdas also includes supplementary materials that Baha'u'llah revealed after the Aqdas was completed. The first of these is the Tablet of Ishraqat, which instructs Baha'is to obey the rulings of the House of Justice and to act according to the rules in the Aqdas. All are to come together, as God wishes, for "Ye are all the leaves of one tree and the drops of one ocean."

Also included are the texts of the Obligatory Prayers. These are the Long Obligatory Prayer, the Medium Obligatory Prayer, the Short Obligatory Prayer, and the Prayer for the Dead.

WRITINGS OF THE BAB

Because Baha'is consider their religion to have begun with the Bab, his writings too are part of Baha'i scripture. His principal work, the Bayan, is a book of holy laws. In setting down these laws the Bab replaces the laws in the Quran. His is clearly a new revelation. The Bab offered new forms of ritual prayer, fasting, and pilgrimage, as well as new forms of tithing, or paying part of one's income to the faith. He also created the 19-month solar calendar, later adapted by Baha'u'llah.

Baha'u'llah based parts of the Aqdas on the Bayan. Much of the Bab's other work was destroyed during the persecution of the Babis. However portions remain, particularly prayers. These are included in Baha'i Prayers.

The Wings of a Bird

In his writings 'Abdu'l-Baha compares humankind to a bird:

The world of humanity has two wings— one is women and the other men. Not until both wings are equally developed can the bird fly. Should one wing remain weak, flight is impossible. Not until the world of women becomes equal to the world of men in the acquisition of virtues and perfections, can success and prosperity be attained as they ought to be.

CHAPTER 5

THE SPREAD OF THE BAHA'I FAITH

From the time Babism was reborn as the Baha'i Faith in 1863, Baha'is actively taught people about the faith. Its leaders sent out believers to spread the word. In its early years most of the growth of the Baha'i Faith took place in Persia, or Iran, where the faith began. However there were early followers in other countries as well. Parts of the Ottoman Empire, Russia, Egypt, India, and Turkmenistan had Baha'i followers. By the 1880s, still within Baha'u'llah's lifetime, the religion had rebounded from a few hundred Babi survivors to many thousands of followers.

THE BAHA'I FAITH IN THE OTTOMAN EMPIRE AND EGYPT

Almost from its beginnings the Baha'i Faith had small groups of followers in parts of the Ottoman Empire, such as Baghdad, where Baha'u'llah spent part of his exile. There was also a community in Egypt. Mostly these communities were made up of Persians who had moved out of Iran. These groups remained small. They were constantly under threat of arrest and exile. So

A view of the mansion at Bahji outside the city of Acre (Akko) where Baha'u'llah lived after the order to keep him in prison was no longer enforced by officials. The Baha'i community has spent many decades beautifying the buildings and grounds where Baha'u'llah spent his final years.

they did little to spread the faith. In the 1890s in Egypt, however, some native Egyptians converted to the Baha'i Faith, creating a small but devoted community.

BRITISH INDIA AND BURMA

By the 1870s there was a small network of Baha'is in northern India. At first it was made up of Indians who had been educated in Persia and had come into contact with the Baha'i Faith there. Later the Baha'i teacher Sulayman Kahn traveled widely in the area and the number of converts grew. He then moved to Burma (present-day Myanmar) and established a community of Baha'is in that country.

THE BAHA'I FAITH IN RUSSIAN TERRITORY

The Baha'i Faith established itself early in the Russian territories that shared a border with Persia. The first was Azerbaijan. Babism had taken root in the Persian-controlled area of Azerbaijan when the Bab was in prison there. Beginning in the 1860s the Babi groups became Baha'is. The religion spread outward into the Russian territories in Azerbaijan and into Ashkhabad, Turkmenistan. Persian immigrants added to its numbers. Then in 1889 some Shii extremists planned and carried out an attack against the Ashkhabad community. To the surprise of the Baha'is the Russian authorities caught the extremists and put them on trial. They were convicted and put in jail for their crime. This was the first time in Baha'i history that a government had not tolerated persecution directed at Baha'is. The Russian territories became a popular place for Baha'i resettlement and the community grew.

True to their social mission the Baha'is in Ashkhabad established schools, a public bath, a hostel (which offers inexpensive rooms to travelers), a clinic, and a hospital. In 1907 they built the first Baha'i house of worship. They were probably the first Baha'i community to elect a council. In so doing they became the model for Baha'i communities to come. The Turkmenistan community flourished until the coming of the communists, who outlawed all religious practice.

THE BAHA'I FAITH IN ITS HOMELAND

Persia was the cradle of Babism and later of the Baha'i Faith. From the 1880s on more and more people there began joining the Baha'i Faith. Many of these new converts were prominent in society. They included Muslim clergy, government officials, and even members of the royal family. They also included members of the Jewish and Zoroastrian faiths. Around this time the religion began to encourage women to become active participants. Wives and daughters joined husbands and fathers. Families began to bring up their children as Baha'is.

From prison in Acre Baha'u'llah kept up a lively correspondence with his followers. To help in administering the growing faith he named four leading Baha'is "Hands of the Cause of God." They helped to organize what was becoming an important national movement.

Baha'is in Persia still suffered persecution at the hands of the Muslim clergy and the Persian government. However they followed Baha'u'llah's teachings and deliberately did not fight back. Baha'u'llah urged his followers to avoid politics but to be loyal citizens of their country. Their steadfastness in the face of persecution won them sympathy and more converts.

'ABDU'L-BAHA

When Baha'u'llah died in 1892 his eldest son, 'Abdu'l-Baha, became the head of the Baha'i Faith. 'Abdu'l-Baha was born in 1844, the same year the Bab declared his mission. His birth name was Abbas Effendi, but early in life he took the name 'Abdu'l-Baha, meaning "Servant of Baha."

From an early age he worked as his father's assistant. As a young man in Adrianople (Edirne) he was responsible for Baha'u'llah's large household, which included not only his mother and sister

The Secret of Divine Civilization

When Baha'u'llah moved out of Acre 'Abdu'l-Baha stayed behind. He attended the local mosque, gave to the poor, and prayed regularly. He fitted in well with the local Muslim society. However he was constantly thinking about the faith and how it might develop in the future. In 1875 he wrote *The Secret of Divine Civilization*, which discussed the modernizing of Iran. In 1886 he wrote *A Traveler's Narrative*, a short history of the Baha'i Faith.

A photograph of 'Abdu'l-Baha as a young man. Like his father before him, 'Abdu'l-Baha never attended school. However he read widely and the Ottoman leaders in Acre respected his scholarship. He married the daughter of a Baha'i merchant in 1873. Together they had seven children, of whom four daughters survived to adulthood. Against the usual Muslim tradition of the time of taking a number of wives, Baha'u'llah had stated that taking only one wife was preferred. Under 'Abdu'l-Baha monogamy became the Baha'i standard.

but also his three half brothers and two half sisters, as well as disciples and other family members. He also served as one of his father's secretaries. His father came to rely heavily on him and referred to him as "the Master."

DIFFICULTIES OF SUCCESSION

Most Baha'is accepted 'Abdu'l-Baha's authority without question. However, he immediately faced problems within his own family. His half brother Muhammad-Ali felt that he himself should have been named leader. In a move that echoed the actions of Mirza Yahya against Baha'u'llah years earlier, he began a campaign to discredit his older brother.

'Abdu'l-Baha's sister, wife, and daughters remained loyal to him, along with an uncle and the uncle's family. However other members of the family sided with Muhammad-Ali. The family infighting did little damage to the loyalty of most followers but it drew the attention of the Turkish authorities to the Baha'is. They reinstated the order of confinement and 'Abdu'l-Baha was once again a prisoner in Acre.

Muhammad-Ali's opposition—which moved from initial acceptance of 'Abdu'l-Baha's leadership, through obstruction, to outright rejection of his authority—only made 'Abdu'l-Baha's own position clearer. 'Abdu'l-Baha continued with the idea that Baha'i followers should remain loyal to the sacred covenant, or agreement, that protected Baha'i unity. This covenant required them to be obedient to their appointed leaders. He denounced Muhammad-Ali and his family as "covenant-breakers" for their disloyalty and ousted them from the faith.

The Baha'i Faith has weathered a number of attempts by individuals to usurp the leadership of the faith, all of which have failed. The Baha'i Faith remains to this day an undivided faith, unlike so many other religions.

THE BAHA'I FAITH SPREADS TO THE WEST

Americans first heard of Baha'u'llah at the Parliament of the World's Religions, a world religion conference held in Chicago in

1893. At about the same time a Syrian merchant named Ibrahim Kheiralla immigrated to the United States. A recent convert to the Baha'i Faith, he offered classes in the Baha'i Faith for anyone who was interested. By 1894 a small Baha'i group organized in Chicago, and the group grew quickly.

One early American convert was Phoebe Randolph Hearst, mother of the millionaire publisher William Randolph Hearst. In 1898 she gathered a group of Baha'i pilgrims, including Kheiralla, and they traveled to Acre to meet 'Abdu'l-Baha.

'Abdu'l-Baha's personality had a great impact on the Americans. His brilliant mind, his charm, and his spiritual understanding led them to compare him to Jesus Christ of Christianity. Mrs. Hearst in particular thought that 'Abdu'l-Baha might be the Messiah. 'Abdu'l-Baha denied this. "No name, no title, no mention, no commendation have I, nor will ever have, except 'Abdu'l-Baha. This is my greatest yearning. This is my eternal life. This is my everlasting glory."

The Hearst party returned to America full of excitement. Their joy and enthusiasm were contagious. In the next few years a steady stream of visitors poured into Acre. By 1900 there were more Baha'i groups, probably numbering around 1,500 people in all, in the West, with groups located in the United States, Canada, Paris, France, and London, England.

THE LEADERSHIP OF 'ABDU'L-BAHA

From Acre 'Abdu'l-Baha continued to direct the faith by letters and through followers across the region. He was an inspired leader. He spoke with great authority about the spiritual and theological aspects of the religion, and his words drew many people to him. He also had a gift for organization. He worked to create the internal structure that would govern the Baha'i Faith. He encouraged Baha'is in different parts of the world to elect local councils.

In 1908 a revolution freed all political prisoners of the Ottoman Empire. 'Abdu'l-Baha was free to leave Acre. He first went to Haifa, where he oversaw the burial of the Bab's remains in a shrine

The Shrine of the Bab on the slopes of Mount Carmel, Israel,
set among the terraced gardens and completed in 2001.

on the slope of Mount Carmel. This was the place Baha'u'llah himself had chosen. It was also the place where the world center of the faith would be established.

'Abdu'l-Baha was in his 60s and his health was not good. However for the first time since his childhood he was not a prisoner. Finally able to travel freely, he began his active ministry. Under his leadership the faith grew and spread and many of its doctrines became established.

'Abdu'l-Baha also wrote his will. It would not be made public until after his death, but it was the blueprint for the growth and spread of the Baha'i Faith. In it he appointed his grandson, Shoghi Effendi, to be the Guardian of the Faith after him. Shoghi Effendi was then only a child. However in him 'Abdu'l-Baha saw the future of the young religion.

'ABDU'L-BAHA'S TRAVELS

'Abdu'l-Baha left Palestine in 1910 bound for Egypt. He was still suffering the effects of his long imprisonment. He stayed in Egypt for several months, resting and recuperating. Then in August 1911 he sailed for France. This was the beginning of a journey that took him throughout the Western world. In the next 28 months, he visited London, England; Paris, France; Stuttgart, Germany; and other European towns and cities as well. Then he sailed for North America.

'Abdu'l-Baha arrived in New York City on April 11, 1912. He traveled the country from coast to coast, visiting more than 40 cities and towns. In Wilmette, Illinois, he laid the cornerstone for the first Baha'i temple in North America. He visited Eliot, Maine, where the Baha'i Faith was presented at the Green Acre retreat. He traveled to Canada and spent time in Montreal.

A NEW WAVE OF BAHA'I BELIEVERS

American and European newspapers gave 'Abdu'l-Baha's travels wide coverage. 'Abdu'l-Baha spoke in churches, universities, peace societies, union halls, and living rooms. It was the first time many Westerners had heard of the Baha'i Faith. For the young

Baha'i communities in Europe, Canada, and the United States it was a wonderful opportunity to meet their leader, listen to his words, and deepen their understanding of both the spiritual and social aspects of the faith. By the end of his tour there was a whole new wave of Baha'i believers.

On his visit to the United States in 1912, 'Abdu'l-Baha attracted Baha'i followers and their families to meetings, discussions, and social gatherings.

IMPACT OF THE AMERICAN COMMUNITY

The American Baha'i community, small as it was, had a great impact on the growth of the faith. The group moved to translate Baha'i literature into English. They wrote brochures explaining the faith directed at Christian readers. They began to set up local councils and to plan for a yearly national convention. Some members traveled to Persia to help with medical and educational work. Others became missionary teachers. They visited existing communities in such places as Hawaii and Germany. In the next few years they visited Japan, Australia, and Brazil, and established communities there.

RETURN TO HAIFA

'Abdu'l-Baha returned to Haifa shortly before the beginning of World War I (1914–18), after more than two years of constant travel. The world situation soon made travel impossible. He turned again to writing letters to his followers. He wrote the *Tablets of the Divine Plan* (1917–18) to Baha'is in North America. In these letters, he urged his followers to begin a campaign to spread the faith not only in the United States and Canada, but also throughout the world.

'ABDU'L-BAHA'S FINAL YEARS

'Abdu'l-Baha's travels had made him a world figure. He was recognized as the leader of an important religious movement. Following the war he was able to use his influence to help Palestine when it faced a famine. The British, who had recently taken control of Palestine, made him a knight of the British Empire in 1920.

'Abdu'l-Baha died on November 28, 1921. His funeral brought together an estimated 10,000 people. They included representatives from the Muslim, Roman Catholic, Greek Orthodox, and Jewish communities of Palestine; also in attendance were the British high commissioner and the governor of Jerusalem. In the 13 years between the end of his confinement as a political prisoner in Acre and his death, he had given the Baha'i Faith world recognition. He had clarified its goals, both spiritual and social. And he had given it an organizational structure that would carry it into the next phase of its existence.

SHOGHI EFFENDI

The terms of 'Abdu'l-Baha's will, which made his grandson Shoghi Effendi the Guardian of the Faith after him, were clear. It named Shoghi Effendi the "sign of God" on earth and directed Baha'is to be obedient to his direction.

Shoghi Effendi Rabbani was born in 1897. He was the son of 'Abdu'l-Baha's daughter and the oldest of 'Abdu'l-Baha's 13 grandchildren. As a teenager he spent his summers as his grandfather's assistant. He graduated from college in Beirut, Lebanon, in 1918

DIRECTING THE BAHA'I FAITH

For the last years of his life, 'Abdu'l-Baha lived in Haifa, directing the work of the Baha'i Faith and corresponding with Baha'i faithful. The faith was now established in many countries around the world and its followers numbered around 100,000. An active student of world affairs, he warned that the peace accords that had ended World War I would not end conflict, and that the Balkan nations would continue to be unstable. Many of his predictions proved to be true. He insisted, however, that they were not divine revelation but simply rational thinking.

'Adbu'l-Baha returning to his home on Haparsim Street in Haifa, Israel.

and became his grandfather's chief secretary. In 1920 he went to study at Oxford University in England. He wanted to improve his English so that he could translate Baha'i scriptures. He was at Oxford when his grandfather died.

SHOGHI EFFENDI ASSUMES LEADERSHIP

Shoghi Effendi was 24 years old when he became leader of the Baha'i Faith. Most Baha'is accepted him gladly as his grandfather's true heir. The young man faced a huge task. 'Abdu'l-Baha had grown old serving the religion. He had seemed like a father to his followers. Shoghi Effendi was young with modern ideas and a Western education. His leadership would be quite different.

It took several years for Shoghi Effendi to take control of his many new duties. At first he worked day and night, almost to the verge of collapse. Over the course of his 36 years as Guardian he sent more than 17,500 letters. He kept up with the progress of all the existing Baha'i communities. The situation in the Middle East, where the religion was still under attack, required his response. During this time he translated a great many of Baha'u'llah's writings into English.

THE SCRIPTURAL CANON

One of Shoghi Effendi's greatest contributions to the faith was his interpretation and translation of the works of Baha'u'llah and 'Abdu'l-Baha. His grandfather's will had named him the sole authority for interpreting Baha'i works. Shoghi Effendi was fluent in Persian and Arabic as well as English. His ability to translate the scriptures into English was a major factor in the growth of the American Baha'i community. Over the years of his guardianship he was the principal translator of most of the Baha'i scriptures. He also wrote an important history of the first 100 years of the Baha'i Faith, *God Passes By*.

A CLEAR VISION FOR THE FAITH

Shoghi Effendi had a clear vision for the progression of the faith. They were handed down to him from 'Abdu'l-Baha and founded upon the original writings of Baha'u'llah, especially in the Kitab-i-Aqdas. Two aspects of his leadership were especially important to him in this context. From the beginning of his time as its leader he focused on developing its administration and on spreading the faith worldwide.

Shoghi Effendi dedicated his life almost entirely to achieving the goals he had been given for the Baha'i Faith. Unlike his grand-

Shoghi Effendi became leader of the Baha'i Faith at the age of 24. He worked for 36 years as Guardian until his unexpected death in London in 1957.

father he did not attend the local mosque. He sent representatives to local affairs rather than going himself. Also unlike his grandfather he did not visit Baha'i communities in other countries. In his many letters he referred to his position as Guardian rather than to himself personally.

THE ADMINISTRATIVE PLAN

Among Shoghi Effendi's many accomplishments as Guardian was his development of a systematic administration based upon the writings of both Baha'u'llah and 'Abdu'l-Baha. The faith had grown too large to be administered by just one person or even one group. He therefore introduced an organizational system. To aid the spiritual assemblies that made up the faith he introduced requirements for voting, membership rolls, and national centers to administer such matters as translating and publishing. A better network of Baha'i communities emerged.

Shoghi Effendi created an International Baha'i Council to help him in his work. He extended the Hands of the Cause of God by adding a group of devoted believers to this directing council. Their job was to help the national spiritual assemblies achieve their goals and to advance and protect the faith. Finally he established support boards to assist the Hands.

THE TEACHING PLAN

Once the assemblies were functioning smoothly Shoghi Effendi turned his attention to teaching. This was to be the principal means for spreading the faith around the world. Under his direction a seven-year plan (1937–44) was produced. It called on Baha'is to settle in all the American states, Canadian provinces, and Latin American countries where there were no Baha'is. The Baha'is who undertook this challenge were known as "pioneers." American Baha'is were also to work toward finishing the Baha'i temple at Wilmette, Illinois (near Chicago).

A second seven-year plan (1946–53) directed Baha'is in North America to continue their work in the Americas. They were also to help Europe recover after World War II (1939–45) and to re-

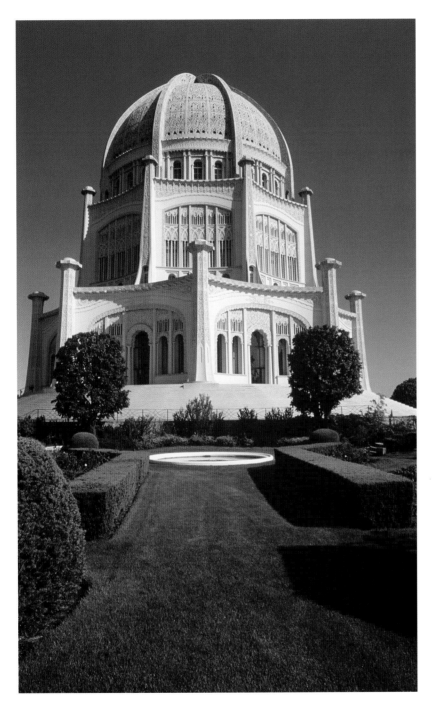

'Abdu'l-Baha laid the cornerstone for the house of worship in Wilmette, Illinois, in 1912 during his visit to America. It was the first Baha'i temple built in the West.

establish the faith there. Other national assemblies received attainment targets as well.

In 1953 Shoghi Effendi launched a 10-year global crusade. Its purpose was to establish the faith throughout the world in all the countries where it was not yet established.

THE BAHA'I WORLD CENTER AND SHOGHI EFFENDI'S LEGACY

Under Shoghi Effendi the Baha'i World Center in Haifa, Israel, became a reality. First he purchased the mansion at Bahji, near Akko (formerly Acre), where Baha'u'llah had lived at the end of his life. Later he purchased more land and created gardens. He did the same with land around the Shrine of the Bab and directed the erection of a golden-domed building over the shrine. Shoghi Effendi saw to the construction of an international archives building nearby. In it are kept Baha'i scriptures and relics. He approved a master plan for the development of a center that would eventually be a complex of buildings, gardens, and shrines. It would be the place that Baha'is from all over the world could identify as the center of their religion.

Shoghi Effendi died in London in 1957 and is buried there in the Great Northern Cemetery. According to Baha'i laws Baha'is are buried within one hour's traveling of the place where they died.

THE HANDS OF THE CAUSE OF GOD

In 1957 Shoghi Effendi died unexpectedly of natural causes in London. He had not left a will. 'Abdu'l-Baha had obviously meant the institution of Guardian to be handed down within the family, but Shoghi Effendi and his wife had no children. He had not named a successor. There would be no more guardians. Nor had he left specific instructions for the direction of the faith after his death. The 10-year plan was only half completed. Shoghi Effendi's death was a serious loss to Baha'is worldwide.

Shortly before his death, however, Shoghi Effendi had named the Hands of the Cause of God "Chief Stewards" of the faith. He had given them the authority to see that plans for the future were carried out. They therefore took on the responsibility of carrying the faith forward.

Under their stewardship the faith continued to grow and spread, and Shoghi Effendi's blueprint for a global religion took on substance. The 10-year plan moved forward on schedule, eventually achieving its goals. The Hands of the Cause of God also took steps toward establishing the Universal House of Justice, to which they handed over their authority in 1963.

CONTINUED GROWTH

Shoghi Effendi worked all his life to spread the faith throughout the world. To a large extent he succeeded. The plans he initiated exceeded their goals. In 1935, before the first plan, there were 139 spiritual assemblies worldwide and Baha'is lived in 1,034 localities. By 1953 those numbers had increased to 670 spiritual assemblies and 2,700 localities.

Shoghi Effendi did not live to see the completion of his 10-year crusade. However his plan vastly increased the Baha'i Faith's geographical presence in the world. By 1963 Baha'i had 4,437 spiritual assemblies and was established in 14,437 localities. The number of national assemblies increased from 10 in 1935 to 56 in 1963. During Shoghi Effendi's time as Guardian the number of people professing the Baha'i Faith had reached more than 400,000. In the next half century it would grow even more.

CHAPTER 6

BAHA'I BELIEF AND WORSHIP

Baha'i worship has few formal structures. There are no priests, ministers, mullahs, or rabbis. There is no liturgy and there are no rituals. As in most other areas of the religion a great deal is left up to the individual. Baha'is guide themselves along the path that leads them to spiritual truth. The whole of Baha'i life is a spiritual quest.

THE SPIRITUAL JOURNEY

Baha'u'llah writes that all creation reflects divine attributes. Yet of all creation, human beings are particularly special. Only humans can reflect all of the attributes of God. "Alone of all created things, man hath been singled out for so great a favor, so enduring a bounty," says Baha'u'llah. Human lives have two aspects, he says—the material or animal side, and the spiritual side; what makes a person truly human is his or her spiritual nature.

According to Baha'u'llah people cannot find true happiness in worldly things: "The world is but a show, vain and empty, a mere nothing, bearing the semblance of reality." He tells his followers that instead of grasping at material things they must try to

The establishment of the Baha'i World Center was the 'Fulfillment of the Tablet of Carmel'. The building of the Center confirmed Baha'u'llah's vision for the slopes of Mount Carmel in Haifa, Israel.

God's Wondrous Bounties

In *Gleanings* Baha'u'llah writes:

Should a man wish to adorn himself with the ornaments of the earth, to wear its apparels, or partake of the benefits it can bestow, no harm can befall him, if he alloweth nothing whatever to intervene between him and God, for God hath ordained every good thing, whether created in the heavens or in the earth, for such of his servants as truly believe in Him. Eat ye, O people, of the good things which God hath allowed you, and deprive not yourself from his wondrous bounties. Render thanks and praise unto him, and be of them that are truly thankful.

Best Beloved of All Things

The best beloved of all things in My sight is Justice; turn not away there from if thou desirest Me, and neglect it not that I may confide in thee. By its aid thou shalt see with thine own eyes and not through the eyes of others, and shalt know of thine own knowledge and not through the knowledge of thy neighbor. Ponder this in thy heart: how it behooveth thee to be. Verily [truly] justice is my gift to thee and the sign of my loving-kindness. Set it then before thine eyes.

(In Baha'u'llah, *Hidden Words*, 2.)

form the divine power within them. At the same time people are not to deny themselves the good things of the world in the name of religion. The goal is moderation and thankfulness, not extreme self-denial.

DIVINE ATTRIBUTES

Certain attributes give humans spiritual power. According to Baha'u'llah these include justice, love, trustworthiness and truthfulness, purity and chastity, actions, and service to others. People who seek to develop these qualities within themselves are following a spiritual path.

JUSTICE AND LOVE

Baha'u'llah particularly stresses the importance of justice. Baha'is must always be fair in their treatment of others and respect the rights of all. They should also show the same consideration to themselves. "Be fair to yourselves and to others, that the evidences of justice may be revealed, through your deeds, among Our faithful servants," he says.

TRUE SPIRITUAL LOVE

Love is also very important. 'Abdu'l-Baha points out that there are many kinds of love: love of family, of country, of institutions, of one's own race. However, all of these are imperfect. In loving their own country, for example, some people may find fault with other countries. True spiritual love is universal and unlimited. It reaches out to everyone. Baha'u'llah also praises other qualities that grow out of love for humanity. These qualities include kindness, friendliness, compassion, consideration, patience, and generosity.

TRUSTWORTHINESS

According to Baha'i scripture trustworthiness is the basis of all human interaction. Without trustworthiness people cannot truly conduct the business of life. Prosperity is built on trust. Along with this goes truthfulness, which 'Abdu'l-Baha calls "the foun-

Baha'is in Zambia singing and clapping during a period of devotion before their study circle begins in the home of a local community member.

dation of all human virtues." A truthful person is always sincere and deals honestly with others.

PURITY AND CHASTITY

Purity and chastity are required of all Baha'is. However, they are warned not to become puritanical or self-denying. They should strive for moderation in matters of dress, language, and amusements. They should be modest, pure, and temperate, and should keep their thoughts pure. They are to be chaste, but not to an extreme. And they should develop healthy lifestyles: Baha'is are discouraged from smoking, and are forbidden to use alcohol or mind-altering drugs unless prescribed by a physician for a medical condition.

WORK AND SERVICE

"Let deeds, not words, be your adorning," Baha'u'llah writes. "The essence of faith is fewness of words and abundance of deeds." One way that Baha'is show their faith is in service to others. Baha'is donate their time to teaching or community projects. In the Baha'i Faith it is a duty to have a trade or profession. Baha'is are asked to use their skills to enrich both their own lives and the lives of those around them. Work is a form of worship.

SHORT OBLIGATORY PRAYER

There are three obligatory prayers. A Baha'i may choose any one of them. The Short Obligatory Prayer is one such prayer; it is to be said sometime between noon and sunset:

I bear witness, O my God, that Thou has created me to know Thee and to worship Thee. I testify, at this moment, to my powerlessness and to Thy might, to my poverty and to Thy wealth.

There is none other God but Thee, the Help in Peril, the Self-Subsisting.

BAHA'I LAWS AND OBLIGATIONS

To Baha'is discipline is an essential and integral part of reaching any goal, and spiritual progress requires spiritual discipline at all times. Baha'u'llah offered his followers a number of laws to help them work toward unity and harmony. Among these laws are social laws, such as the laws for marriage, and obligations for achieving spiritual growth. These include prayer, reading of scriptures, meditation, and fasting.

PRAYER

Prayer is one of the most important obligations of a Baha'i. Every Baha'i is expected to pray daily and to meditate. Baha'is may create their own prayers, or they may use any of the many prayers written by the Bab, Baha'u'llah, and 'Abdu'l-Baha, which have been translated into many languages. The only requirement is that one of the daily prayers must come from the obligatory prayers of Baha'u'llah.

MUSIC, SCRIPTURE, AND MEDITATION

Prayers may be spoken, chanted, or sung. Baha'u'llah approved of music, and according to 'Abdu'l-Baha, "The art of music is divine and effective. It is the food of the soul and spirit." Baha'i hymns are words from the scriptures set to music. Baha'u'llah also instructs his followers to read scripture and to meditate. This duty requires them to read from the scriptures twice a day, morning and evening, and to think about the essential meaning. The act of meditating helps to turn the individual's mind away from the world and toward spiritual things. According to 'Abdu'l-Baha, "When you meditate you are speaking with your own spirit. In that state of mind you put certain questions to your spirit and the spirit answers: the light breaks forth and the reality is revealed."

FASTING

Another Baha'i obligation is fasting. During the Baha'i month of Ala, from March 2 to March 20, Baha'is fast from sunrise to sunset, as Muslims do during the holy month of Ramadan. This is a time of spiritual preparation for the New Year, which begins on March 21. According to Shoghi Effendi the fast is a period of meditation and prayer that leads to spiritual renewal. The Baha'i fast symbolizes their need to turn away from the materialistic world and toward God.

MARRIAGE

In the Baha'i Faith marriage is recommended but not required. According to 'Abdu'l-Baha, "Baha'i marriage is the commit-

Loving Companions and Comrades

The Baha'i Faith requires that both the man and the woman consent freely to the marriage and that they have each obtained the consent of their respective parents. 'Abdu'l-Baha emphasizes the importance of the couple's knowing each other well. They should "exercise the utmost care to become thoroughly acquainted with the character of the other . . . Their purpose must be this: to become loving companions and comrades and at one with each other for time and eternity."

ment of the two parties one to the other, and their mutual attachment of mind and heart." The Baha'i Faith recognizes the importance of the physical bond of marriage but stresses that the spiritual side is more important. Since the time of 'Abdu'l-Baha's leadership, monogamy between a man and a woman is the only form of marriage permitted. Baha'is consider the institution of marriage to be God-given and vital to society.

The marriage ceremony has no set form. Couples may write their own service. They may incorporate any local customs they wish. The only set part of the ceremony is that they must exchange a vow before witnesses. That vow is, "We

Three newlywed couples having their wedding photos taken at the entrance plaza of the Baha'i Terraces on Mount Carmel, Haifa.

will all, verily, abide by the Will of God." Divorce is strongly discouraged. However, it may be permitted as a last resort after a year of separation and attempts to reconcile. If the couple still cannot agree, permission to divorce is granted.

FAMILY LIFE AND CHILDREN

Baha'is place great importance on family. The family is the source of spiritual growth for the individual. It is also the foundation of society. The family provides a spiritual atmosphere for children to grow and learn. The education of children is central to Baha'i belief.

The Baha'i Faith teaches that the most important social function of marriage is that of raising children. Parents are to create an atmosphere of love and harmony in their home. In such an atmosphere all members of the family can flourish. Parents must set the example for their children. They must be truthful, free of prejudice, and just. In their relationship with each other they must demonstrate the equality of men and women.

THREE KINDS OF EDUCATION

Baha'is recognize three kinds of education. Physical education provides the skills that enable people to survive. Education in reading and writing, arts and sciences, allows people to participate in the world and to enjoy the benefits of knowledge. Spiritual education and respect for all living things makes individuals complete human beings.

Education of children is a religious duty in the Baha'i Faith. Education begins at,

Kindness to Animals

The physical sensibilities and instincts are common to animal and man . . . the poor animals cannot speak . . . therefore one must be very considerate toward animals and show greater kindness towards them than to man. Educate the children in their infancy in such a way that they may become increasingly kind and merciful to the animals.

(In 'Abdu'l-Baha, *Tablets of 'Abdu'l-Baha.*)

Children's Prayer

O God! Educate these children. These children are the plants of Thine orchard, the flowers of Thy meadow, the roses of Thy garden. Let Thy rain fall upon them; let the Sun of Reality shine upon them with Thy love. Let Thy breeze refresh them in order that they may be trained, grow and develop, and appear in the utmost beauty. Thou art the Giver. Thou art the Compassionate.

(In 'Abdu'l-Baha, *Baha'i Prayers.*)

A moral education class for children in a Baha'i school in Columbia. Baha'i children learn about the meaning and teachings of their faith from an early age.

or even before, birth, as parents prepare themselves to bring up their children according to Baha'i teachings. A child's early years are the most important in developing good character. "While the branch is green and tender, it can easily be made straight," writes 'Abdu'l-Baha. When children are old enough, they should go to school. Baha'i writings stress the importance of educating girls, because they will be the first teachers of the next generation.

GROWING STRONG IN FAITH

'Abdu'l-Baha says that parents must tend their children as a gardener tends tender young plants, seeing that they grow strong in faith. Parents should applaud and praise their good deeds and qualities, and dispense discipline if necessary. However, punishment is to be based on reason. It is never permitted to strike or belittle a child, as these actions damage the child's character. Children are the future and hope of the world. They must always be treated with respect and dignity.

THE COVENANT

The Baha'i Faith does not ask its members to follow any specific creed or doctrine. Every Baha'i is free to understand the scriptures for him- or herself. However all Baha'is live by a single unifying principle. This is the covenant, or Baha'i spiritual agreement.

The covenant is the unifying force that holds the Baha'i Faith together. "The power of the Covenant will protect the Cause of Baha'u'llah from the doubts of the people of error," wrote 'Abdu'l-Baha. "It is the fortified fortress of the cause of God and the firm pillar of the religion of God. Today no power can conserve the oneness of the Baha'i world save the Covenant of God."

The covenant leaves each follower of the Baha'i Faith free to interpret the scriptures. At the same time it prohibits any individual from claiming that his or her interpretation is the only correct one. Only the writings of Baha'u'llah and the interpretations of 'Abdu'l-Baha and Shoghi Effendi are authoritative.

People become Baha'is by agreeing to abide by the covenant. There is no conversion ceremony for those joining from another faith, and no other requirement. Similarly there is no confirmation ceremony. When young people reach the age of 15, which is considered the age of consent, they may choose to join the fellowship. They simply agree to abide by Baha'i laws and are admitted to the community.

DEATH AND BURIAL

In the Baha'i Faith death marks the point at which the soul passes to the next world. As such, it is "the bearer of gladness" for the believer, according to Baha'u'llah. There is no way to prove that there is life after death. However, Baha'is believe that life does not end with death; the soul is eternal. 'Abdu'l-Baha writes, "To consider that after the death of the body the spirit perishes is like imagining that a bird in a cage will be destroyed if the cage is broken, though the bird has nothing to fear from the destruction of the cage."

As the vessel that has housed the soul during life, the body is treated with respect. Funeral ceremonies are dignified. There is a specific prayer for funerals. Otherwise, the ceremony may be as simple or elaborate as the family wishes. Cremation is forbidden. Bodies are buried so that they may naturally become part of the earth. Baha'i laws require that Baha'is be buried within an hour's journey of the place of death.

The Baha'i Faith teaches that in this world believers can help, in the next world, those who have died by performing good deeds in their name or through prayer.

Prayer of Intercession for the Dead

O my God! Thou forgiver of sins, bestower of gifts, dispeller of afflictions!

Verily, I beseech Thee to forgive the sins of such as have abandoned the physical garment and have ascended to the spiritual world. O my Lord! Purify them from trespasses, dispel their sorrows, and change their darkness into light. Cause them to enter the garden of happiness, cleanse them with the most pure water, and grant them to behold Thy splendors on the loftiest mount.

(In 'Abdu'l-Baha, *Baha'i Prayers*.)

Dr. Rodney Clarken (on the left), a Baha'i and one of the original signatories of the Earth Keeper Covenant, helping to collect "e-waste" from offices and homes. The Baha'i community is committed to environmental policies in their training and programs.

THE BAHA'I CALENDAR

All of the world's calendars are associated in some way with religion. The calendar the secular world uses is actually the Christian calendar, which begins with the birth of Jesus Christ. However there are also Jewish and Islamic calendars that date from important events in those religions. Baha'i religious life is organized

MONTHS OF THE BAHA'I YEAR

The Baha'i year begins with the spring equinox, March 21, which was the traditional New Year's Day in Iran. The months are named after spiritual or divine qualities.

Each year has 19 months of 19 days. In order to bring the number of days to 365, four additional days are inserted before the last month of the year. These days are called Ayyam-i-Ha. Baha'is celebrate this time by inviting others to their homes for Ayyam-i-Ha parties and by giving gifts, visiting the sick, and performing community service.

Baha'i Month	Translation	Begins
Baha	Splendor	March 21
Jalal	Glory	April 9
Jamal	Beauty	April 28
Azamaat	Grandeur	May 17
Nur	Light	June 5
Rahmat	Mercy	June 24
Kalimat	Words	July 13
Kamal	Perfection	August 1
Asma	Names	August 20
Izzat	Might	September 8
Mashiyyat	Will	September 27
Ilm	Knowledge	October 16
Qudrat	Power	November 4
Qawl	Speech	November 23
Masa'il	Questions	December 12
Sharaf	Honor	December 31
Sultan	Sovereignty	January 19
Mulk	Dominion	February 7
Ala	Loftiness	March 2

around a solar calendar originally developed by the Bab and adapted by Baha'u'llah.

THE 19-DAY FEAST

Every 19 days, at the beginning of each Baha'i month, is a 19-Day Feast. If possible all Baha'is attend. The feast is the cornerstone of each local Baha'i community activity.

The feast is actually a meeting with three parts. The first part of the meeting is devoted to prayers and the reading of scripture. This is the Baha'i worship service. The second part is an administrative session. People give reports on Baha'i activities in the area. Individuals raise issues that are important to them and the members of the community discuss them. Finally there are refreshments. In smaller communities the 19-Day Feast is held in someone's home. In larger areas the feast may be held in the Baha'i centers.

In some places Baha'is meet weekly for devotions and fellowship. They usually meet on Sundays, when most people do

A reflection meeting at a local Baha'i center in Ntambo, Zambia. Baha'is regularly meet for prayers and scripture readings. The second part of these gatherings is a discussion on the administration and progress of their work in the local area.

not have to work. Weekly devotions consist of reading from the works of Baha'u'llah or other founders and reciting prayers.

BAHA'I HOLY DAYS

Baha'is observe nine holy days, which commemorate events in Baha'i history. Feasts such as Navruz and Ridvan are celebrations. Baha'is gather to read scripture, consult, and share fellowship. During Ridvan, the "Most Great Festival," they also elect new leaders. The Passing of Baha'u'llah and the Bab's martyrdom are solemn occasions when Baha'is pray and read scriptures. If possible they abstain from work on their holy days.

HOUSES OF WORSHIP

Most Baha'i services take place in homes or in Baha'i centers. However, Baha'i houses of worship are a very important part of the Baha'i Faith. Houses of worship are called Mashriqu'l-Adhkar, or "Dawning Place of the Praises of God." At the present time there are seven houses of worship worldwide—one for each continent. They are in Wilmette, Illinois, as well as New Delhi, India; Kampala, Uganda; Sydney, Australia; Frankfurt, Germany; Panama City, Panama; and Apia, Samoa. Currently there are plans to build a Baha'i house of worship in Tehran, Iran; Santiago, Chile; and Haifa, Israel. Specific sites have been chosen in these cities but no significant building work has taken place.

Houses of worship are open for devotional services that people of all religions—or no religious background—may attend. Services are nondenominational. They consist only of readings and prayers from all of the world's religions. Some of these have been set to music and may be sung by a choir. There are no sermons.

All Baha'i houses of worship have nine sides and a dome. These architectural features are symbols that the Baha'i Faith is open to all religious traditions. They show

BAHA'I HOLY DAYS

Navruz (New Year)	March 21
Ridvan—first day	April 21
Ridvan—ninth day	April 29
Ridvan—12th day	May 2
The Bab's Declaration	May 23
Passing of Baha'u'llah	May 29
Martyrdom of the Bab	July 9
Birth of the Bab	October 20
Birth of Baha'u'llah	November 12

that people may come from many directions and through many doors, but gather in recognition of one God.

In addition to the existing houses of worship, the Baha'i Faith owns property in other countries around the world, where it will eventually build other houses of worship. More than 100 locations have been designated as suitable. In time Baha'is envision that the Mashriqu'l-Adhkars will be the centers of community life. Around them they will build administrative centers, schools, colleges, clinics, homes for the elderly, and other community services. In this way the house of worship will be the central focus of communities that come together in peace and harmony and service to God.

The Baha'i house of worship outside Sydney, Australia, is the first Baha'i temple built in the South Pacific. It was dedicated in September 1961.

CHAPTER 7

THE BAHA'I COMMUNITY

The Baha'i Faith is organized around the Baha'i community. In the community Baha'is put their faith into practical action. Through the community Baha'is implement the social, educational, and spiritual goals of their religion.

THE BAHA'I ADMINISTRATIVE ORDER

The laws and rules of the Baha'i Faith and Baha'i institutions together form the Baha'i Administrative Order. The Administrative Order is the way that the Baha'i Faith is organized. To Baha'is, however, it is much more than a system of organization. Its foundations and guiding principles were laid down by its founders; it is therefore sacred. Baha'is understand that the institutional framework of their faith puts words into actions, a central aim of the faith. Moreover, Baha'is believe that their model of community will eventually provide a working model for the construction by humankind of a global society. Baha'is therefore work diligently to support it and follow its rules as the best hope for bringing peace and prosperity to all humanity.

The Universal House of Justice at the Baha'i World Center in Haifa, Israel. Its members, elected by all the national assemblies, are the highest authority in the Baha'i world.

BAHA'I INSTITUTIONS

Unlike most other organized religions such as Judaism, Christianity, and Islam, the Baha'i Faith has no priests or clergy. It has no professional religious scholars who interpret the scriptures for believers. Baha'u'llah taught that a priesthood or clergy was not necessary. In earlier times, when few people could read and write, they needed a professional priesthood. They needed someone who could tell them what the Bible or the Quran said and help them to understand scripture. However the Baha'i Faith is a religion for the modern age. Modern society can give everyone the opportunity to read and write. This means that people can read and understand the scriptures for themselves; a mature humanity does not need a professional clergy.

However, in most organized religions religious professionals have another important function. They administer the business of the religious body. They coordinate its local, regional, national, and international activities. They serve as a resource for religious matters. Many have publishing houses that produce literature for and about the religion. Others have business offices that oversee mission efforts or schools. In the Baha'i Faith the administrative structure performs these functions.

THE SPIRITUAL ASSEMBLIES

Whenever an area has at least nine adult Baha'i members, those nine or more people hold an annual election for the local spiritual assembly, the governing body for the faith in that area. It is responsible for supervising the activities of the faith. Its duties include spreading the word about the Baha'i Faith, running its educational programs, local publicity and publishing, holding devotional services and meetings, finances, and counseling on matters of faith.

A country with a sufficient number of local spiritual assemblies may form a national spiritual assembly. Elected delegates attend an annual convention at which the national spiritual assembly is elected. National spiritual assemblies oversee and coordinate the activities of the local assemblies.

Baha'is hold yearly elections in April during the festival of Ridvan. All voting is by secret ballot. Baha'i rules prohibit nominations or campaigning. Each member simply lists nine names on his or her ballot. When the ballots are counted the nine individuals with the highest number of votes are elected to the assembly. Their term begins immediately after the election and they serve for one full year.

The teachings of Baha'u'llah ask Baha'is to consider the qualities of the people they elect and to choose "only those who can best combine the necessary qualities of unquestioned loyalty, of selfless devotion, of a well-trained mind, of recognized ability and mature experience." However, Baha'u'llah encouraged his followers to give preference to minority members.

Tamun Kosep (in the center), a traditional chief and treasurer of the first Local Spiritual Assembly of Madina, Papua New Guinea, flanked by other Baha'is at a community celebration in 2004.

THE UNIVERSAL HOUSE OF JUSTICE

The Universal House of Justice is the international governing body of the Baha'i Faith and the highest authority in the Baha'i world. It has authority for guarding and developing the faith, and according to the Baha'i texts, is explicitly described as "protected from error." This authority was handed down directly from

Voting in 1998 to elect the Universal House of Justice, the Supreme Governing Council. Members of the Universal House of Justice are elected for five-year terms by the members of all the national assemblies.

GOALS OF THE PLANS

An important function of the Universal House of Justice is the growth and development of the faith around the world. Since it began it has produced several plans for spreading the faith. These have been the Nine-Year Plan (1964–73); the Five-Year Plan (1974–79); the Seven-Year Plan (1979–86); the Six-Year Plan (1986–92); the Three-Year Plan (1993–96); the Four-Year Plan (1996–2000); the Twelve-Month Plan (2000–01); and the Five-Year Plan (2001–06). The plans are crucial to Baha'i administration because they set the goals for the spreading of the faith. The goals of the different plans have included:

Spreading the faith around the world and increasing its membership.

Establishing and improving the functioning of the Baha'i administrative order in all parts of the world and helping local communities to take on more responsibility for reaching Baha'i goals.

Encouraging the individual spiritual development of all Baha'is as well as their participation in all aspects of the Baha'i community.

Improving the quality of Baha'i community and family life, especially education.

Increasing the involvement of Baha'is in society, particularly with regard to social and economic development.

Increasing the translation, production, distribution, and use of Baha'i literature.

Spreading the message of Baha'u'llah to all parts of society and all minority groups.

Developing the Baha'i World Center.

Building new houses of worship.

Working with international organizations such as the United Nations and its divisions.

Baha'u'llah. It has the power to set up rules for the Baha'i community and to rule on religious matters not covered in the writings of Baha'u'llah, 'Abdu'l-Baha, or Shoghi Effendi. It is located in Haifa, Israel.

IMPLEMENTING THE COVENANT

In the Kitab-i-Aqdas and related writings Baha'u'llah spelled out the system of institutions through which the covenant he had created would be implemented. First, authority to interpret the sacred texts was vested solely in 'Abdu'l-Baha, who was designated the Center of Covenant. Second, 'Abdu'l-Baha was further charged with the responsibility for the affairs of the Baha'i community; and third, in due course, as circumstances permitted, a three-level system of Houses of Justice would assume full authority for the administration of any disputes.

The instructions that Baha'u'llah himself had left for creating the Universal House of Justice were later developed by 'Abdu'l-Baha and Shoghi Effendi. The Universal House of Justice finally came into being during the Baha'i World Congress in 1963, when the first members were elected. All Baha'is must follow the decisions of the Universal House of Justice. However, any decision may be amended at a later time by another ruling. In this way the faith can grow and change with new times and circumstances.

RESPONSIBILITIES OF THE UNIVERSAL HOUSE OF JUSTICE

The tasks of the Universal House of Justice are similar to those of the local and national spiritual assemblies but it also works to:

- promote peace among nations
- ensure that no organization within the Baha'i community abuses its privileges
- safeguard the rights of individuals within the Baha'i Faith
- develop the Baha'i World Center and its administrative processes
- resolve disputes within the Baha'i World Center
- preserve the Baha'i Faith's sacred texts

THE BAHA'I WORLD CENTER

The Baha'i World Center is in Haifa, Israel. It contains one of the holiest shrines of the Baha'i Faith, the Shrine of the Bab, and also its important administrative buildings. These include:

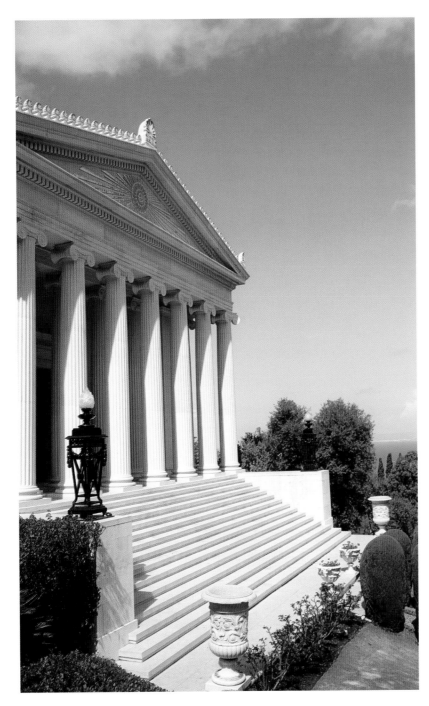

The International Archives Building containing relics and
scriptures is part of the administrative buildings that form the
Baha'i World Center in Haifa, Israel.

- The Seat of the Universal House of Justice
- The International Teaching Center
- The International Baha'i Archives
- The Center for the Study of the Texts

A community health worker nurse in Zambia. Health programs are an important part of Baha'i commitment to the community at large and their work is often combined with United Nations' health projects.

The Shrine of the Bab houses the Bab's remains. Baha'u'llah himself chose the site of the shrine on the slope of Mount Carmel, which he called the "mountain of God." 'Abdu'l-Baha is also buried there. The houses and grounds where the central figures of the Baha'i Faith lived are nearby. They have been restored and are open to Baha'i pilgrims. Baha'i holy places also include the Shrine of Baha'u'llah at Bahji, just outside Akko, and the mansion where Baha'u'llah spent his last years. The Shrine of the Bab, the mansion at Bahji, and the complex of administrative buildings are surrounded by carefully tended gardens. The World Center complex has luxuriant gardens, streams, and fountains on 19 terraces. The World Center is a place of pilgrimage for Baha'is from around the world.

The World Center continues to develop in the 21st century. In 2001 new gardens opened at the Shrine of the Bab and became a major tourist attraction. A Baha'i library is also planned.

APPOINTED INSTITUTIONS

Besides the Baha'i Faith's elected institutions, there are appointed positions. These mostly operate out of the International Teaching Center in Haifa.

Because no further Hands of the Cause of God could be appointed after Shoghi Effendi's death, the Universal House of Justice created the International Teaching Center in 1973. The job of the International Teaching Center is to coordinate the Continental Boards of Counselors in promoting and protecting the faith. It also assists the Universal House of Justice in creating its long-term plans. Members are appointed for five-year terms.

THE RIGHTS OF MINORITIES

In the words of 'Abdu'l-Baha, "In the estimation of God, all men are equal. There is no distinction of preference for any soul, in the realm of His justice and equity . . . This variety in forms and coloring, which is manifest in all the kingdoms, is according to creative wisdom and hath a divine purpose." All forms of prejudice are expressly forbidden.

As an article of their faith Baha'is work to see that the rights of all minorities are protected. Shoghi Effendi wrote, "Every organized community enlisted under the banner of Baha'u'llah should feel it to be its first and inescapable obligation to nur-

Searching Out the Truth

When Baha'is come together for consultation they must do so in the spirit of love and harmony, according to the writings of 'Abdu'l-Baha. He continues:

They must then proceed with the utmost devotion, courtesy, dignity, care and moderation to express their views. They must in every matter search out the truth and not insist upon their own opinion, for stubbornness and persistence in one's views will lead ultimately to discord and wrangling and the truth will remain hidden. The honored members must with all freedom express their own thoughts, and it is in no wise permitted for one to belittle the thought of another, nay, he must with moderation set forth the truth, and should differences of opinion arise, a majority of voices must prevail, and all must obey and submit to the majority.

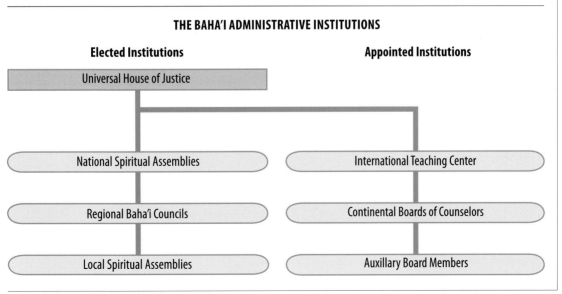

THE BAHA'I ADMINISTRATIVE INSTITUTIONS

Elected Institutions	Appointed Institutions
Universal House of Justice	
National Spiritual Assemblies	International Teaching Center
Regional Baha'i Councils	Continental Boards of Counselors
Local Spiritual Assemblies	Auxillary Board Members

ture, encourage, and safeguard every minority belonging to any faith, race, class, or nation within it."

CONSULTATION

Key to carrying out the Baha'i Administrative Order is the process of consultation. Consultation involves a frank and honest but loving exchange of opinions by members of a group. The goal of consultation is to achieve complete agreement. The result is the fruit of the group's collective wisdom. All decisions in the Baha'i Faith are made by consultation.

As Baha'is carry out consultation, the goal is not to find a majority opinion. It is to find a unanimous one. If there is no unanimous decision the majority opinion must be respected. The idea of consensus carries over into all aspects of Baha'i life. It is a tool not only within the Baha'i community but also in school, the family, and the workplace.

Two girls work together at a Bahá'í agricultural school in Tanzania.

POWER AND AUTHORITY

In the Baha'i Faith institutions, not individuals, receive power and authority. An individual who is elected to a position in a local or national spiritual assembly does not have any special power and does not consider him- or herself to be a "leader of the Baha'i community." The institution is the leader. It, not the individuals in it, hold the power.

As much as possible Baha'i institutions pass authority down to the next level, toward the local assemblies, rather than keeping control themselves. For example it is the responsibility of the Universal House of Justice to see that the faith advances and expands. However, as soon as a national assembly has enough experience, it takes over that responsibility in its area. When a local assembly is strong enough the national assembly encourages it to take over that function. In this way all individual Baha'is share the power and authority of the faith. Baha'is rely on the Administrative Order and the institutions of the Baha'i Faith to give form and structure to their communities and their daily lives.

The National Spiritual Assembly of the Baha'is in Cuba meeting for consultation at the National Baha'i Center in Havana. The goal of consultation is to achieve complete agreement through an honest and thoughtful exchange of opinions.

BAHA'IS AND THEIR COMMUNITY

The institutions of the Baha'i Faith support and sustain the Baha'i community as a whole. Worship, service, teaching, and fellowship all take place within the structure of the Administrative Order. Baha'is understand that in becoming members of the Baha'i Faith they have joined a community, not merely a congregation. As members of a community they have an obligation to work together, to support one another, and to do all that they can to help the community not only survive but thrive. No matter how small their local communities may be, Baha'is also understand that they are part of a worldwide community of believers that stretches around the globe, held together by the sacred laws and institutions of their faith.

CHAPTER 8

THE BAHA'I FAITH TODAY

In 1992, 100 years after the passing of Baha'u'llah, Baha'is from around the world met for the Second Baha'i World Congress. An estimated 30,000 Baha'is gathered in New York City for four days. New York, "the City of the Covenant," was where Western audiences first heard 'Abdu'l-Baha proclaim the covenant of Baha'u'llah on his North American tour in 1912. The Baha'is who gathered there in 1992 were among the largest and most diverse group ever to come together in one place.

Satellite links broadcast the conference to groups meeting in Buenos Aires, Argentina; Sydney, Australia; New Delhi, India; Nairobi, Kenya; Panama City, Panama; Bucharest, Romania; Moscow, Russia; Singapore; and Western Samoa. A highlight of the conference was the participation of the Russian Baha'is. After decades of suppression the Russian Baha'i community, one of the earliest, has been rebounding since the fall of the Soviet Union.

The members of the Universal House of Justice spoke to the wide-flung conferences from their center in Haifa, Israel. The conference celebrated the growth of the faith and the unity in diversity made possible by the Baha'i covenant.

One of the entrances to the Shrine of the Bab in Haifa, Israel.

 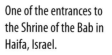

SPREADING THE FAITH

The Baha'i Faith began in Iran in the middle of the 19th century and has spread to 236 countries and territories throughout the world. The largest Baha'i communities now exist in Africa, southern Asia, and Latin America. These communities, wherever they have formed, have followed the educational programs appropriate to the Baha'i way of life. Baha'is acknowledge both the animal and spiritual character of man. Although they consider man's spiritual nature to be superior to his animal character the Baha'is are far from neglecting man's animal needs. They do not practice rigorous asceticism. Their religious message in regard to the body and external things is one of moderation and grateful enjoyment. They see material realities as gifts from God and enjoy them as divine blessings. So part of their overall teaching is enjoyment of and gratitude for the wonderful things of life.

BRINGING FORTH A RICH HARVEST

Many of life's blessings, Baha'is realize, are the result of human effort. Part of their teaching mission is to instruct people on how to work effectively. They want to show people how their own

GROWTH IN THE INSTITUTIONS OF THE BAHA'I FAITH

	1954	1963	1968	1973	1988	1994	2001	2008
National Spiritual Assemblies	12	56	81	113	149	172	182	236
Local Spiritual Assemblies	708	3,379	5,902	17,037	19,486*	17,780*	11,740*	10,000*
Localities where Baha'is Reside	3,117	11,092	31,883	69,541	112,137	119,276	127,381	100,000*

*The drop in the number of localities and local spiritual assemblies, which started in 1979, is due to reorganizations in which local assemblies have been consolidated to take in more than one town or village.

efforts can help themselves and their neighbors. Baha'is spread their faith not by preaching, but by example. They show their appreciation for the material world by teaching people how to function better within it: Teaching better farm methods or training them in technical trades.

RESPECT, EQUALITY, AND SENSITIVITY

The Baha'i way of educating is also spiritual. Baha'is show their concern for others by fostering proper social behavior: treating others with respect, showing fairness in business practices, promoting equality of races, and cultivating sensitivity for other religions. There is also a great respect for those who maintain their own beliefs; there are no professional missionaries attempting to convert others to this particular religious way of life. It is through

A Baha'i study circle in Canada. Baha'is spread their faith through example, drawing in others who begin to appreciate their way of life.

the example of how they live, the positive attitudes of their judgments, and their openness to others that Baha'is believe they spread their faith. They simply move into a new area and "pioneer" through positive example, encouraging those who become interested their way of living. Instead of appointed missionaries who attempt to gain new followers by preaching, Baha'is draw others to their faith by showing the appeal of their way.

A Bahá'í teaching a scripture class at a public school in Australia in November 2002.

"FIRESIDE" GATHERINGS

Baha'is do not attempt to draw people to their religion by showing them impressive churches or promoting elaborate ceremonies and rituals. Their approach is simple and informal. Baha'is might invite friends or neighbors who show interest in the Baha'i Faith to a "fireside." This simple event, if it may be called an event at all, is a small study group that discusses the fundamental Baha'i beliefs. At such gatherings Baha'is share the basics of their faith and recount their personal journeys of spiritual growth. They are convinced that this ordinary, uncomplicated, approach is successful, since most Baha'is have come to their religion through such "firesides."

TEACHING

Baha'is have not created elaborate religious rituals. Nor have they developed a detailed legal code of conduct. The emphasis of their religion is placed on teaching and learning. Baha'is who have matured in their spiritual journeys are most competent to teach others. Yet this has not tempted Baha'is to develop elaborate school systems for training in their Baha'i Faith. Their education-

Women training at the Barli Development Institute in Indore, India. The project offers agricultural training as well as health and nutrition programs. Development centers such as these encourage sustainable livelihoods for local people.

al program follows simple down-to-earth learning procedures. Most young people receive their early learning from their parents. In communities where mothers provide the principal care for their children, mothers will also be the first teachers. They are generally the ones who teach fundamental values and attitudes of mind. Mothers show their children the value of fairness, consideration, truthfulness, respect, compassion, and other basic Baha'i virtues.

Baha'is want believers to learn how to meet different challenges, to develop effective working abilities, and to improve their homes and communities by helping their neighbors. Believers should contribute to the vitality of the places where they live by helping their neighbors and their communities, and they should also develop schools or training centers in these areas. The effectiveness of such centers for training workers in job-related skills and in social concern has often been noted in communities throughout the world.

At the celebration of the 100th anniversary of their presence in Germany in September 2005, for example, the mayor of Stuttgart praised the Baha'is for "the respect you pay to other world religions, your openness for people who have different opinions, your message of peace for the world we live in." These are some of the values that are taught by Baha'is by example, through simple accounts of the spiritual journeys of its members at ordinary community gatherings, and in the training schools that in reality teach more than workers' trades and how to adjust to new ways of living.

DEVELOPMENT EFFORTS

Today Baha'i communities run more than 1,714 local development projects around the world. These include schools, adult literacy programs, health clinics, environmental centers, youth programs, women's programs, agriculture, and vocational

Health Care in Africa

In Africa Baha'is have established a network of health-care centers, training villagers in simple techniques of first aid and treatment of common illnesses such as malaria and infant diarrhea, which are often fatal if untreated. The centers enable people to improve the health and well-being of their communities.

CONSULTATION AND COOPERATION

The Universal House of Justice encourages Baha'i support of United Nations' projects. In 1967 Baha'is established a permanent office at the United Nations in New York City. They consult on the United Nations Economic and Social Council and the United Nations Children's Fund (UNICEF). They also work with the World Health Organization (WHO) and the United Nations' Environment Program (UNEP). To help in these joint efforts the Baha'i International Community (BIC) is officially registered with the United Nations as an accredited nongovernmental organization. The BIC has representatives throughout the world who guide the cooperative efforts to find solutions for health, environmental, economic, racial, religious, and cultural problems throughout the world. These representatives call on the national and local Baha'i communities to assist in these joint efforts.

The Baha'i International Community's principal representative to the United Nations addresses the United Nations Millennium Summit in November 2000.

training centers. Most of these projects are undertaken in developing countries.

Baha'is see their social programs as a way to put their faith into action. They believe that social action arises from the best part of the human spirit, and so it is really a spiritual activity. They also see many problems as interconnected. For example they believe that poverty cannot be eliminated until women have full equality, since most of the world's poor are women and children.

In Baha'i-run programs in rural India women in vocational training programs learn marketable skills such as sewing. They also receive instruction in literacy and hygiene. In parts of South America some poor farmers learn modern methods of farming, and others plant trees to restore forests. Others benefit from day-care centers, orphanages, and literacy programs. In a city setting a new vocational institute offers courses in business management, environmental technology, and nutrition.

However Baha'is never teach only skills; they teach Baha'i principles as well. They teach consultation techniques so people can arrive at group decisions that benefit the whole community. Students come to understand the oneness of humanity, giving and sharing, honesty, trustworthiness, and service. They see that education is knowledge and that knowledge is power. Students go home with new ideas that make a difference to the entire community. They may or may not become Baha'is, but the Baha'i principles they learn help them to make their communities a better place to live.

THE BAHA'I FAITH AND THE UNITED NATIONS

Many of the world's chief religions have had difficulties with policies of the United Nations. Many Jewish people judge that in the United Nations there is too much influence from Muslim nations on policies dealing with the state of Israel. Many Muslims view the establishment of the state of Israel as a violation of the territorial rights of Palestinian Muslims. Certain Christian denominations view the United Nations' efforts to control population or to deal with the AIDS crisis as employing immoral methods to find solutions. Often, then, the major religions try to separate themselves from many endeavors of this influential worldwide organization. The Baha'i Faith, in contrast, sees itself as bringing a spiritual foundation to the work of the United Nations that might otherwise, for the sake of not offending a particular religion, declare itself to be independent of all religion.

The Baha'is, influenced by the teachings of Shoghi Effendi, view themselves as adherents of a religion that shares many of the goals of the United Nations. The message of the Baha'i Faith, like that of the United Nations, accentuates the equality of nations and persons, fostering peace and understanding among all people. Its teachings on respect for the body incline Baha'is to be dedicated to improving health care in all parts of the world, and to promote agricultural and technical education that raises the level of life for the unskilled and uneducated everywhere. By its programs, often combined with United Nations' projects, it favors human rights, women's equality, and care for the environment. Its message of respect for other religions likewise tempers religious conflicts in all lands.

PERSECUTION IN RECENT TIMES

Baha'is have often suffered persecution. Sometimes the cause has been their teachings. Their doctrine concerning the unity of humankind, the equality of men and women, and the equality of races, for example, has brought strong criticism from those who view some races as inferior to others. The declaration of the superiority of the Aryan race under Hitler's Nazi regime not only brought persecution and death upon millions of Jews but also persecution of those who, like the Baha'is, defended the equality of all people. Baha'i activities were officially banned from 1937 to 1945. Baha'i communities were dissolved and their literature defending the equality of races was confiscated and destroyed.

Even after World War II (1939–45) Baha'is had trouble gaining official recognition in West Germany. Many Christian churches, both Catholic and Protestant, protested the building of a Baha'i house of worship. They also opposed the declaration of local communities of Baha'is as corporations, which was a require-ment by German law for all religious bodies. The German high court has only lately upheld the judgment that the Baha'i Faith is indeed an independent religion and put an end to these anti-Baha'i efforts.

Similar persecutions took place in Russia after the Commu-nist Revolution. Like all other religious groups the Baha'i Faith as a distinct religion was condemned by the atheistic government, and its gatherings were forbidden. In the 1930s the Stalinist gov-ernment exiled a number of Baha'i officers, especially those who were members of the Hand of the Cause of God. It is only since the fall of Communism in Eastern Europe in the late 1980s that Baha'i communities have been restored to life.

PERSECUTION IN IRAN

The most ferocious persecutions of the Baha'is, however, have taken place in the very birthplace of the Baha'i Faith: Iran. The persecutions began in the 1840s, actions taken by those who considered the Baha'is to be a group of heretical Muslims. This judgment to a great extent explains the Baha'i insistence that the Baha'i Faith is an independent religion.

Certainly the Baha'i Faith grew out of a Muslim context, but the very attitude of Baha'is affirms the positive nature of their religion. They are not critical of other religions. They believe that divine revelation is progressive. The Baha'is believe that they have moved on to a new stage in religion. Theirs is a religion that attempts to see the good in all religions, including the Muslim faith. They do not criticize other faiths, which they believe were products of the time.

Baha'is believe we live in a new era, and particular religious approaches must be open to the more universal context of the world. Baha'is have asked that, in a sense of fairness, the treat-ment of their religion be equal to the favorable treatment given in societies to any recognized religion. In the context of Iran, then, they seek the respect that is accorded to the other main minority religion of Iran, Zoroastrianism.

SUPPRESSION IN IRAN

Unlike Zoroastrians, who also follow a religion that began in Iran and who are a protected minority under Iranian law, Baha'is have no civil rights there. Shortly after the Islamic Republic took control of Iran in 1979, the government began a severe crackdown on Baha'i activities. They seized Baha'i properties and destroyed shrines and cemeteries. Baha'is in jobs under government control were fired, their pensions canceled, and their savings seized. Baha'is were banned from attending Iranian schools and universities. Baha'i schools were banned as well. The authorities arrested prominent members of the 350,000 Iranian adherents to the Baha'i Faith.

In 1983 Iranian authorities arrested 10 Baha'i women and girls. They were accused of teaching the Baha'i Faith to Muslim children. In Iran teaching the Baha'i Faith to Muslims is punishable by death. The authorities offered the women the opportunity to renounce the Baha'i Faith and accept Islam. The women refused and were executed. In all, during this time more than 200 Baha'is were executed as "unprotected infidels," and hundreds more were imprisoned for the "crime" of being members of the Baha'i Faith.

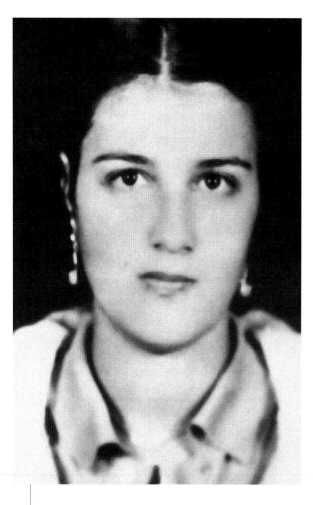

Simin Sabiri, one of 10 Baha'i women executed in Shiraz on June 18, 1983.

UNITED NATIONS' RESOLUTIONS

Many Baha'is fled Iran to escape such persecutions and sought refuge in countries such as Canada and Australia. Outcries from these countries did bring some relief. Since 1985 the United Nations General Assembly has passed resolutions that condemned human rights violations in Iran, some of which specifically mention members of the Baha'i Faith. Australia, for example, where Baha'is, numbering 12,000, have come from Iran and 90 other countries, has consistently supported these United Nations' resolutions, as well as passing national resolutions in 1981, 1997, 1998, and 2000 condemning the Iranian persecutions of Baha'is. Canada, the European Parliament, and the U.S. Congress have also denounced Iran's actions. Discrimination against the Baha'is still continues in Iran particularly in relation to religious freedoms and fair access to education, housing and jobs.

CONTINUING DISCRIMINATION

The United Nations, through its Human Rights Council, has pressured Iran to stop its official persecution of Baha'is. Much of the violent persecution had stopped by the 1990s. However, as recently as 1997 a Baha'i was executed for allegedly converting a Muslim to the Baha'i Faith. Even if the executions of Baha'is in Iran has slowed down, more than 10 years later Baha'is still experience discrimination in education, jobs, housing, travel, and the practice of religion.

CHALLENGES FOR THE FUTURE

The kind of growth that the Baha'i Faith has experienced in the last century brings with it new challenges. One challenge is that of maintaining a unified community. Once a religion composed almost entirely of Muslims of Iranian descent, it now encompasses cultures and peoples of all backgrounds, nationalities, and races. Its followers come from both highly literate and technologically advanced countries and from countries where few people read and write. Baha'i philosophy states that all people are equal in the sight of God, but it recognizes vast differences in opportunity. Still it will be a challenge for the faith, with its limited membership, to encourage a skeptical world that seems torn apart by ethnic, national, and religious strife.

Another challenge is that of participation. With no professional clergy or missionaries and no funding from outside sources, the Baha'i Faith depends entirely on its members to do the work of the

A Source of Power and Vitality

The Universal House of Justice has said that:

(T)he participation of every believer is of the utmost importance, and is a source of power and vitality . . . If every believer will carry out these sacred duties, we shall be astonished at the accession of power which will result to the whole body, and which in turn will give rise to further growth and a showering of greater blessings on all of us.

faith. One of the strongest features of the faith is that everyone is expected to contribute to the community. Its goal is to build a society that will eventually be global in scope.

Most Baha'i communities around the world have begun with the work of pioneers. Over the last few years these new communities have become self-governing and self-sustaining; but there is much work to be done. The young communities are charged not only with governing themselves but also with establishing schools, community centers, and economic development projects as well as continuing to spread the Baha'i message. If the faith is to succeed in its social and spiritual goals it needs the active participation of every member.

Another major challenge is that of dealing with oppression, as problems in Iran have shown. Westerners mostly accept the notion of freedom of religion, but many countries where Baha'i has a presence have established religions and do not welcome other faiths.

TOWARD A NEW WORLD ORDER

More than 100 years ago Baha'u'llah spoke of a "New World Order." Baha'is understand that a time of tremendous upheaval is here. The traditional political, social, and religious solutions seem not to be working; in fact they seem to be pulling society apart. Baha'is believe that out of this time of turmoil will come a time when all humanity is united in love and brotherhood among all peoples. National rivalries will end. Global institutions will be formed. These will help to bring about harmony throughout the world. All war will end. There will be universal peace.

The New World Order will not come into being quickly. However the world is changing. Racial and gender equality is slowly becoming a reality in some parts of the world. Nations are beginning to realize that they are dependent on one another for security and for economic strength. These are all things Baha'u'llah foresaw more than a century ago.

The New World Order of Baha'u'llah covers the entire range of human activity. It is not only a change in the political life of the world, but a revolution in its social, cultural, spiritual, and economic life as well. Baha'is believe that the New World Order is the will of God, and that God wants humanity to be united. They work toward bringing the New World Order about.

BAHA'IS AND WORLD PEACE

Baha'is believe that peace is the result of determination and attitude. Before there can be world peace there must be a will among all nations to have peace on earth. This will comes from spiritual and moral resources.

War continues to be a terrible feature of modern times. All nations speak of the longing for peace, but they seem unable to

The 100th anniversary commemoration of the Portsmouth Peace Treaty of 1905 was held at the Baha'i Center in Eliot, Maine. The treaty ended the Russian-Japanese war of the early 1900s. Representatives were present from the three governments that participated in the treaty signing—Japan, the United States, and Russia.

achieve it. Baha'is identify the barriers to world peace as nationalism, racism, poverty, and religious strife. They believe that the Baha'i Faith offers a practical model for breaking down these barriers.

THE BAHA'I FAITH AS A MODEL FOR WORLD SOCIETY

Baha'u'llah teaches that all of humanity is one people. He wrote that the time had come to unify all the people in the world into one global society. Barriers of race, creed, class, worship, and nationalism will fall. They will give way to a single, unified civilization.

In order for this new world civilization to come into being, say Baha'is, people must follow the principles Baha'u'llah laid out. They must recognize that humankind is one and eliminate

Baha'i youth dance workshops held in Malaysia. The participants were invited to wear the traditional dress of their ethnic background to reflect the unity of all races.

all forms of prejudice. They must bring about full equality for women. They must recognize the essential oneness of all religions. They must eliminate extremes of poverty and of wealth.

People must see that science and religion are both forces for good and reconcile the two; they must achieve a balance between technology and nature. There must be universal education. People must maintain a high standard of personal conduct, with service, generosity, kindness, and goodwill toward others. Finally, there should be a world federal system, governing all. To many such goals sound impossible. Yet every day Baha'is put them into practice.

In the 21st century the Baha'i world continues to grow and spread. Since the 1950s, when there were about 200,000 Baha'is worldwide, adherence to the faith has increased 25-fold to more than 5 million people. In the Baha'i Faith people of all racial, ethnic, and national backgrounds come together in cooperation to pursue the goals of their faith. In creating harmony within diversity, Baha'is believe that they stand as a model for the world.

COUNTRIES AND TERRITORIES WHERE
THE BAHA'I WORLD COMMUNITY HAS A PRESENCE

Africa

Algeria
Angola
Benin
Botswana
Burkina Faso
Burundi
Cameroon
Cape Verde Islands
Central African Republic
Chad
Comoros
Democratic Republic
of the Congo
Djibouti
Egypt
Equatorial Guinea
Eritrea
Ethiopia
Gabon
Gambia
Ghana
Guinea
Guinea-Bissau
Ivory Coast
Kenya
Lesotho
Liberia
Libya
Madagascar
Malawi
Mali
Mauritania
Mauritius
Morocco

Mozambique
Namibia
Niger
Nigeria
Republic of the Congo
Reunion
Rwanda
Saint Helena
Sao Tome and Príncipe
Senegal
Seychelles
Sierra Leone
Somalia
South Africa
Sudan
Swaziland
Tanzania
Togo
Tunisia
Uganda
Western Sahara
Zambia
Zimbabwe

Americas

Anguilla
Antigua and Barbuda
Argentina
Aruba
Bahamas
Barbados
Belize
Bermuda
Bolivia
Brazil

Canada
Cayman Islands
Chile
Colombia
Costa Rica
Cuba
Dominica
Dominican Republic
Ecuador
El Salvador
Falkland Islands
French Guiana
Grenada
Guadeloupe
Guatemala
Guyana
Haiti
Honduras
Jamaica
Martinique
Mexico
Montserrat
Netherlands Antilles
Nicaragua
Panama
Paraguay
Peru
Puerto Rico
Saint Kitts–Nevis
Saint Lucia
Saint-Pierre and
Miquelon
Saint Vincent and the
Grenadines
Suriname

COUNTRIES AND TERRITORIES WHERE
THE BAHA'I WORLD COMMUNITY HAS A PRESENCE (continued)

Trinidad and Tobago
Turks and Caicos
United States
U.S. Virgin Islands
Uruguay
Venezuela

Asia

Afghanistan
Azerbaijan
Bangladesh
Bhutan
Cambodia
China
India
Indonesia
Japan
Laos
Malaysia
Maldives
Mongolia
Nepal
Myanmar (Burma)
Pakistan
Philippines
Singapore
South Korea
Sri Lanka
Taiwan
Tajikistan
Thailand
Timor-Leste
Turkmenistan
Uzbekistan
Vietnam

Australasia

American Samoa
Australia
Cocos (Keeling) Islands
Cook Islands
Fiji
French Polynesia
Guam
Kiribati
Marshall Islands
Micronesia
Nauru
New Caledonia
New Zealand
Niue
Northern Mariana Islands
Palau
Papua New Guinea
Samoa
Solomon Islands
Tokelau Islands
Tonga
Tuvalu
Vanuatu
Wallis and Futuna Islands

Europe

Albania
Andorra
Armenia
Austria
Belarus
Belgium
Bosnia and Hertzegovina
Bulgaria

Channel Islands
Cyprus
Czech Republic
Denmark
Estonia
Faeroe Islands
Finland
France
Georgia
Germany
Gibraltar
Greece
Greenland
Hungary
Iceland
Ireland
Isle of Man
Italy
Liechtenstein
Lithuania
Luxembourg
Malta
Monaco
Netherlands
Norway
Poland
Portugal
Romania
Russia
San Marino
Slovakia
Slovenia
Spain
Sweden
Switzerland

COUNTRIES AND TERRITORIES WHERE
THE BAHA'I WORLD COMMUNITY HAS A PRESENCE (continued)

Ukraine
United Kingdom
Yugoslavia

Middle East
Bahrain
Brunei
Gaza Strip
Iran

Iraq
Israel
Jordan
Kuwait
Lebanon
Oman
Qatar
Saudi Arabia
Syria

Turkey
United Arab Emirates
West Bank
Yemen

(data from Baha'i Organization, 2008.)

An international conference at the Bahá'í House of Worship
in Apia, Samoa.

FACT FILE

Worldwide Numbers

The Baha'i Faith consists of around 5 million followers in 236 different countries and territories.

Holy Symbol

This nine-pointed, three interlocking triangle symbol represents the completeness and unity of humankind.

Holy Writings

The writings of the Bab and Baha'u'llah are seen as divine revelations and form the backbone of the faith.

Holy Places

These are the tomb of Baha'u'llah and the shrine of the Bab, which are both situated in Haifa, Israel.

Founders

It was founded in 1863 by Mirza Husayn Ali Nuri or Baha'u'llah. It grew out of the Shii branch of the Muslim faith. The followers believe that Baha'u'llah is the most recent in the line of messengers from God. The main message is that the time has come for all of humanity to unite.

Festivals

Baha'is observe nine holy days, which commemorate events in Baha'i history. They include: Navruz, the spring equinox and the traditional New Year's Day in Iran (March 21); Ridvan, which marks the time that Baha'u'llah spent in the garden of Ridvan and his announcement that he was the prophet spoken of by the Bab (April 21–May 2); the feast of the ascension of Baha'u'llah (May 29); the birth of the Bab (October 20); and the birth of Baha'u'llah (November 12).

BIBLIOGRAPHY

'Abdu'l-Baha, *Baha'i Prayers*. London: Baha'i Publishing Trust, 1979.

'Abdu'l-Baha, *Paris Talks*. London: Baha'i Publishing Trust, 1979.

'Abdu'l-Baha. *Tablets of Abdul-Baha Abbas*. Chicago : Bahai Publishing Society [1909-19]. Ann Arbor, Mich.: University Microfilms International, 1980.

Baha'u'llah. *Gleanings from the Writings of Baha'u'llah*. Translated by Shoghi Effendi. Wilmette, Ill.: Baha'i Publishing Trust, 1976.

Baha'u'llah, *Kitab-i-Iqan*. Translated by Shoghi Effendi. Wilmette, Ill.: Baha'i Publishing Trust, 1950.

Baha'u'llah. *The Hidden Words of Baha'u'llah*. Translated by Shoghi Effendi. Wilmette, Ill.: Baha'i Publishing Trust, 1985.

Browne, Edward Granville. *Materials for the Study of the Babi Religion*. Cambridge, England: Cambridge University Press, 1918.

H. M. Balyuzi, *The Bab*. Oxford UK: George Ronald, 1973.

Momen, Moojan. *A Short Introduction to the Baha'i Faith*. Oxford: Oneworld Publications, 1997.

Nabil, *The Dawn-Breakers*. Translated by Shoghi Effendi. Wilmette, Ill.: Baha'i Publishing Trust, 1996.

Shoghi Effendi, *God Passes By,* 3rd edition. Wilmette, Ill.: Baha'i Publishing Trust, 1973.

The Baha'i Organization. Available online. URL http://news.bahai.org/media-information/statistics/ Accessed on December 8, 2008. Population facts and figures for the Baha'i community.

WEB SITES

Further facts and figures, history, and current status of the religion can be found on the following Web sites:

www.bahai.org
The official presence of the Baha'i Faith on the Internet. It is a comprehensive body of authentic material presented by the Baha'i International Community.

www.bahai.us
The official Web site of the Baha'is of the United States of America.

www.planetbahai.org
A broad-based resource on the Baha'i Faith.

www.bbc.co.uk/religion/religions/bahai
A guide to the Baha'i Faith, including its history, beliefs, holy days, and family values.

www.mediabahai.org
A free interactive online service operated and owned by the Bahá'í International Community.

FURTHER READING

Baha'is, The. New York: Office of Public Information, Baha'i International Community, 2002.

Baha'u'llah. *The Hidden Words of Baha'u'llah.* Translated by Shoghi Effendi. Wilmette, Ill.: Baha'i Publishing Trust, 1932, 1985.

Baha'u'llah: The Central Figures, Vol. I. New York: Baha'i International Community, Office of Public Information, 2001.

Baha'u'llah, and Frederick Glaysher. *The Universal Principles of the Reform Bahai Faith.* Rochester, Mi.: Reform Bahai Press, 2008.

Breuilly, Elizabeth, Joanne O'Brien, Martin Palmer, and Martin E. Marty. *Religions of the World: The Illustrated Guide to Origins, Beliefs, Traditions & Festivals.* New York: Checkmark Books/Facts On File, 2005.

Buck, Christopher. *Paradise and Paradigm: Key Symbols in Persian Christianity and the Baha'i Faith.* [Studies in the Bab and Baha'i religions, v. 10]. Albany, N.Y.: State University of New York, 1999.

Danesh, John, Seena Fazel, and Paul Slaughter. *The Baha'i Faith in Words and Images.* Oxford: Oneworld, 2007.

Faizi, Gloria. *The Baha'i Faith: An Introduction.* New Delhi: Baha'i Pub. Trust, 1990.

Garlington, William. *The Baha'i Faith in America.* Lanham, Md.: Rowman & Littlefield, 2008.

Gouvion, Colette, and Philippe Jouvion. *The Gardeners of God: An Encounter with Five Million Bahai's.* Oxford: Oneworld, 1993.

Hain, Robin and Juliet Mabey. *Treasury of Baha'i Prayers, Selections from the Writings of Baha'u'llah, the Bab, and 'Abdu'l-Baha.* Oxford: Oneworld Publications, 1999.

Hatcher, William S., and J. Douglas Martin. *The Baha'i Faith: The Emerging Global Religion.* Wilmette, Ill.: Baha'i Pub, 2002.

Holley, Horace. *Baha'i: The Spirit Of The Age.* Eastbourne, UK: Gardners Books, 2007.

Momen, Moojan, and Moojan Momen. *The Baha'i Faith: A Beginner's Guide.* Oneworld beginners' guides. Oxford: Oneworld, 2008.

O'Brien, Joanne, Martin Palmer, and Joanne O'Brien. *The Atlas of Religion.* Berkeley: University of California Press, 2007.

Smith, Peter. *A Short History of the Baha'i Faith.* Oxford, England: Oneworld, 1997.

Vickers, Patrick. *The Baha'i Faith.* Oxford: Eastbourne, UK: Oneworld, 1994.

Warburg, Margit. Baha'i. *Studies in contemporary religions.* Salt Lake City, Utah: Signature Books, 2003.

GLOSSARY

'Abdu'l-Baha—The Baha'i name of Abbas Effendi, son of Baha'u'llah and leader of the Baha'i Faith, 1892–1921.

Acre—A prison city in Palestine where Baha'u'llah was imprisoned; now the city of Akko in Israel.

Administrative Order—Rules that govern the Baha'i Faith.

Adrianople—The former name of Edirne, the city in European Turkey to which Baha'u'llah was banished.

Aqdas—The Kitab-i-Aqdas, the Most Holy Book.

atheists—People who do not believe in God.

Ayyam-i-Ha—The name for the days added to the Baha'i calendar to bring the total to 365 or 366 (leap year).

Azalis—Supporters of Mirza Yahya (Subh-i-Azal) against Baha'u'llah for leadership of the Baha'i Faith.

Azerbaijan—An area of northwestern Iran where the Bab was imprisoned; now an independent country.

Bab, the—Ali Muhammad, a religious leader in Iran who founded the Babi Faith. His religious name means "gate."

Babi Faith—Or Babism. The religious movement founded by the Bab.

Badasht—A town in Iran; the scene of an important Babi conference.

baha—An Arabic word meaning "glory."

Baha'i International Community—The Baha'i organization that works with the United Nations.

Baha'i World Center—The center of the Baha'i Faith, located in Haifa, Israel.

Baha'u'llah—The Baha'i name for Mirza Husayn Ali Nuri, founder of the Baha'i Faith. It means "Glory of God."

Bahji—The last home of Baha'u'llah, and a place of Baha'i pilgrimage.

banishment—Sending someone away from his or her home country as a punishment.

bastinado—A beating on the soles of the feet with sticks or rods, used as punishment or torture.

Bayan—The name of the book of rules written by the Bab.

Book of Certitude—The book in which Baha'u'llah describes divine progression (see KITAB-I-IQAN).

calligraphy—A kind of stylized handwriting.

Chihriq—The name of the prison in which the Bab was kept.

clergy—Ministers, priests, or rabbis of a faith.

convert—Someone who leaves one religion and joins another; to change religions.

covenant—The Baha'i spiritual agreement and pledge taken by all Baha'is.

covenant-breakers—Those expelled from the faith for failing to accept the covenant of Baha'i unity.

divine messenger—A person sent by God to teach humanity. In the Baha'i Faith divine messengers include all founders of the world's great religions and the Bab.

Edirne—Formerly Adrianople. The city in European Turkey to which Baha'u'llah was banished.

exile—To force someone to live away from his or her country.

Festival of Ridvan—The 12-day celebration of Baha'u'llah's declaration.

fireside—The name for a Baha'i gathering in which the religion is taught.

Gleanings from the Writings of Baha'u'llah—A collection of works by Baha'u'llah, read as scripture.

Guardian of the Faith, guardianship—Term for a leader of the Baha'i Faith; the position held by Shoghi Effendi.

Haifa—The city in Israel where the Baha'i World Center is located.

Hands of the Cause of God—Group of leaders appointed to assist in Baha'i administration.

heresy—A religious belief that goes against established church doctrines.

heretic—Someone denounced by the church for holding beliefs contrary to established faith.

Hidden Imam—In Shii Islam, the 12th religious leader in a line established by the prophet Muhammad. The Hidden Imam is expected to come again to lead the Muslim people.

Hidden Words, The—A book of instruction written by Baha'u'llah (*see* KALIMAT-I-MAKNUNIH).

huququ'llah—"Right of God"; the voluntary wealth tax paid by Baha'is to support the faith.

imam—Term used by Muslims for a religious leader.

infidel—An unbeliever; someone who does not believe in the predominating religion.

intercession—Prayer offered on behalf of another.

Iqan—The Kitab-i-Iqan, the Book of Certitude.

Islam—The religion begun by the prophet Muhammad and widely practiced in the Middle East.

jihad—"Striving" for one's religion. Often translated as "holy war."

Kalimat-i-Maknunih—The Hidden Words, a book written by Baha'u'llah.

Kitab-i-Aqdas—Most Holy Book, a book of rules for the Baha'i Faith written by Baha'u'llah.

Kitab-i-Iqan—Book of Certitude, a book written by Baha'u'llah.

Letters of the Living—The name for the first 18 converts to the Babi Faith, so named by the Bab.

Mahdi—Arabic name for the Hidden Imam.

Maku—Fortress in Azerbaijan where the Bab was imprisoned.

martyrdom—Death or suffering because of one's beliefs.

Mashriqu'l-Adhkar—A Baha'i house of worship.

Mirza Yahya—Half brother of Baha'u'llah who plotted against him (*see* SUBH-I-AZAL).

monogamy—The practice of having only one wife.

mosque—Muslim house of worship.

Most Holy Book—The Aqdas, or Baha'i book of divine rules (*see* KITAB-I-AQDAS).

Muhammad—The name of the prophet who proclaimed Islam.

Muhammad, Siyyid—Supporter of Mirza Yahya against Baha'u'llah.

Mulla Husayn—An early follower of the Bab; one of the Letters of the Living.

mullah—A Muslim trained in religious law.

New World Order—A coming time of universal peace and unity under Baha'i principles.

19-Day Feast—The first day of each Baha'i month when Baha'is gather as a community to read scripture, discuss issues, and share refreshments.

obligatory—Required, as a prayer or a fast.

Ottoman Empire—The empire of the Turks, ca. 1300–1918, encompassing parts of Europe, Asia, and Africa.

penal colony—A place in which people who have committed crimes are confined.

Persia—The former name of Iran.

pioneers, pioneering—In the Baha'i Faith, the tradition of moving to other localities or countries to establish the faith there.

progressive revelation—The unfolding of God's plan for humanity through the teachings of different religious leaders over the ages.

Quddus—A follower of the Bab; one of the Letters of the Living.

Quran—The holy book of Islam.

Ridvan—An Arabic word meaning "paradise"; the garden on an island in the Tigris River where Baha'u'llah addressed his followers.

Ridvan Declaration—Baha'u'llah's sharing with his followers the revelation that he is a divine messenger.

shah—The name for the ruler of Persia (Iran).

Shaykh Tabarsi—A shrine used as a fortress by Babis when they were attacked.

Shia—A Muslim sect, dominant in Persia/Iran.

Shoghi Effendi—The grandson of 'Abdu'l-Baha; Guardian of the Baha'i Faith, 1921–57.

Siyah-Chal—The Black Pit, a prison where Baha'u'llah was held.

Siyyid—The title of respect used by Muslims who trace their ancestry back to the prophet Muhammad.

spiritual assembly—The name for an organized group of Baha'is.

Subh-i-Azal—Mirza Yahya, half brother of Baha'u'llah.

Sufis—Islamic mystics.

Tablet of Ishraqat—Part of the Aqdas; letter of instruction from Baha'u'llah to the Baha'i faithful.

Tahirih—A woman poet and follower of the Bab; one of the Letters of the Living.

12th Imam—In Twelver Shia, the One Who Would Arise; the Hidden Imam or Mahdi.

Twelver Shia—A form of Islam with the belief that the 12th Imam will return.

Universal House of Justice—The highest governing body in the Baha'i Faith.

Vahid—An early follower of Babism.

INDEX

A

'Abdu'l-Baha (1844–1921) 13, 53, 71–73, 111; on the covenant 95; on death 95–96; death of 78; on education 94; in Haifa 78, 79; his travels 76–77; the leadership of 74–75; on love 88; on marriage 91–92; on music and meditation 91; principles of the Baha'i Faith 21; on racial equality 111–112; on truthfulness 89–90; the writings of 20, 63–65

Abraham 14, 57

Acre, Baha'u'llah's imprisonment at 51, 58, 71

administration of the faith 82

Administrative Order 102–113

Ali-i-Barfurush, Muhammad 29

animals, kindness to 93

Azalis 51

B

Bab, the ["the Gate"] (1819–50) 11, 14, 24; the Bab appears 27; and Baha'u'llah 40–41; death of 35; declaration of 28; imprisonment and trial 31–32, 33; and the "Letters of the Living" 28–29, 32; the message of 29–30; under house arrest 30–31; writings of 66–67

Babism 24, 28–37, 40–48

Badasht conference 32–33, 41, 42

baha (Greatest Name symbol) 20

Baha'i Administrative Order 102–113

Baha'i calendar 60, 98–99

Baha'i International Community (BIC) 122

Baha'i World Center, Haifa 8, 20, 84, 108–110

Baha'u'llah (1817–92) 13, 14, 16, 24, 38, 86–88; banishment of 43–44; conversion to Babism 40–41; death of 51–53; God's revelation to 16, 42, 46–47; imprisonment at Acre 51, 58, 71; persecution 42–43; the proclamation of 48–51; withdrawal to the mountains 45–46; writings of 20, 46, 51, 54–63

Bayan, the 66–67

"Book of Certitude" (Kitab-i-Iqan) 46, 54, 57–58

Browne, Edward Granville 52

Buddha 14

burial 95–96

Burma, the Baha'i Faith in 70

C

chastity 90

children in the Baha'i Faith 93–95, 121

cleanliness 61

communism 70, 125

community: organization of 102–113; service to others 90; unity in 20–21

confession, prohibition of 60

consultation 112

conversions 19

Cormick, Dr. William 33

covenant, the 73, 95, 108

D

death 95–96

development projects 121–123

divine attributes 88–90

divine messengers 14–15, 16, 57–58

divorce 60

E

economic matters, 'Abdu'l-Baha on 65

education 61, 93–94, 119–121

Egypt, the Baha'i Faith in 68–70

equality: racial 19, 20, 64–65, 111–112; sexual 33, 65, 93

Europe, the Baha'i Faith in 74, 76–77, 78, 82–84, 124–125

F

family life 93–95, 121

fasting 60, 91

festivals: holy days 100; 19-Day Feast 99–100; Navruz 100: Ridvan Festival 46–47, 100, 105

"fireside" gatherings or study groups 118

ABOUT THE AUTHOR

The late **Paula R. Hartz** was a teacher and a textbook editor, and specialized in writing nonfiction and educational materials for elementary and secondary school students. She is the author of *Daoism, Native American Religions, Shinto, Taoism,* and *Zoroastrianism,* all from Chelsea House's World Religions series.

ABOUT THE SERIES EDITORS

Martin Palmer is the founder of ICOREC (International Consultancy on Religion, Education, and Culture) in 1983 and is the secretary-general of the Alliance of Religions and Conservation (ARC). He is the author of many books on world religions.

Joanne O'Brien has an M.A. degree in theology and has written a range of educational and general reference books on religion and contemporary culture. She is co-author, with Martin Palmer and Elizabeth Breuilly, of *Religions of the World* and *Festivals of the World* published by Facts On File Inc.

PICTURE CREDITS